THAT DAY IN DALLAS

Lee Harvey Oswald Did NOT Kill JFK

ROBERT K. TANENBAUM
Foreword by Robert J. Groden

An Imprint of Skyhorse Publishing, Inc.

Copyright © 2025 by Robert K. Tanenbaum
Foreword copyright © 2025 by Robert J. Groden

All Rights Reserved. No part of this book may be reproduced in any manner without the express written consent of the publisher, except in the case of brief excerpts in critical reviews or articles. All inquiries should be addressed to Regnery Publishing, 307 West 36th Street, 11th Floor, New York, NY 10018.

Regnery Publishing books may be purchased in bulk at special discounts for sales promotion, corporate gifts, fund-raising, or educational purposes. Special editions can also be created to specifications. For details, contact the Special Sales Department, Regnery Publishing, 307 West 36th Street, 11th Floor, New York, NY 10018 or info@skyhorsepublishing.com

Regnery® and Skyhorse Publishing® are registered trademarks of Skyhorse Publishing, Inc.®, a Delaware corporation.

Visit our website at www.skyhorsepublishing.com.
Please follow our publisher Tony Lyons on Instagram @tonylyonsisuncertain

10 9 8 7 6 5 4 3 2 1

Library of Congress Cataloging-in-Publication Data is available on file.

Hardcover ISBN: 978-1-5107-8365-2
eBook ISBN: 978-1-5107-8366-9

Cover design by Brian Peterson

Printed in the United States of America

Contents

Foreword by Robert J. Groden   v

Introduction   vii

PART ONE: CIRCLE OF TRUST

Chapter 1: I Know This Much Is True   1

Chapter 2: Right from the Very Start   13

PART TWO: THE TRUTH SHALL SET YOU FREE

Chapter 3: Higher Calling   41

Chapter 4: Best Case Scenario: Trusting Frank S. Hogan   49

Chapter 5: Another One for the Books: Trusting Richard Sprague   55

PART THREE: TRUTH BE TOLD

Chapter 6: Entering into Evidence   61

Chapter 7: Making My Case   75

Chapter 8: Decentralized Intelligence: Government
    Duplicities and Complex Contrivances   91
Chapter 9: Evidentiary Culmination   113

Appendix 1: Truman Memo   125
Appendix 2: McCone Letter   126
Appendix 3: Rangers at Pointe du Hoc   129
About the Author   131

FOREWORD

by Robert J. Groden

That Day in Dallas: Lee Harvey Oswald Did Not Kill JFK. November 22, 1963, was that day that changed the world.

As former staff photographic consultant to the HSCA, I first met Robert Tanenbaum in early 1977 at his office in Washington, DC. He had just been hired by the House Select Committee on Assassinations after many successful years as a prosecutor for the New York County District Attorney's office in Manhattan. We became friends and have remained so for nearly six decades.

I was initially impressed with his openness in discussing his realization that the Warren Commission Report had been little more than a cover-up. Bob wanted to find the truth—whatever that turned out to be. We worked together on issues concerning the medical evidence in the case and the problems connecting the visual evidence with the written record.

Bob was uniquely qualified for his job due to his history as a successful assistant DA and his record of winning cases. He was able to evaluate the evidence against Lee Harvey Oswald through the lens of a prosecutor. He was committed to truth and invested countless hours trying to get justice in this case.

That Day in Dallas covers Bob's involvement with the investigation from the inside of the issues. He explains to a new generation the workings and failings of the HSCA. Those with a thirst for knowledge about the Kennedy case can learn from his story, which is unique.

Those of us who were fortunate to have worked with him will never forget the experience. Had Bob remained in his position with the HSCA, the final report would have been much stronger than it was.

Thank you, Bob, for your bravery. And your devotion to the truth.

—Robert J. Groden

Introduction

The government sought closure; the people demanded the truth. Portents of a winter of despair were about to dawn.

When the government engages in an official inquiry into a matter of extreme public concern, the government is obligated, in good faith, to search for truth without fear or favor and report its findings to the people. Pursuant to this self-evident truth, the Warren Commission (WC) failed in its attempt to engage in a thorough, comprehensive, and professional investigation into all aspects of the assassination of President John F. Kennedy.

One of the central reasons for its abject shortcomings was that the Federal Bureau of Investigation (FBI), its primary responsible investigative agency, had prior to the WC investigation already concluded that Lee Harvey Oswald (LHO) was the lone gunman and had acted without foreign intervention. The resulting WC alleged investigation was a sham and a charade that short-circuited a legitimate probe.

Credible witnesses with vital evidence that contradicted the preconceived FBI conclusion were ignored. It gives credence to the public perception that the WC report was less than sincere in fulfilling its mission.

Moreover, because of the overwhelming impact that the assassination had on our country, coupled with the WC faux investigation, overall government credibility suffered a stunning blow.

Part of the impetus of finally writing this book is to:

1. Expose what happened.
2. Explore understanding of how and why it happened.

A compelling exploration of an emotional and intensely passionate journey, with *That Day in Dallas: Lee Harvey Oswald Did Not Kill JFK*, I have set out to present clear and convincing powerful pieces of corroborative trustworthy evidence that will overwhelmingly demonstrate the truth of exactly what occurred in Dealey Plaza during the assassination of JFK and the injuries to Governor John Connally.

The Kennedy assassination was a colossal outrage. It fractured our fundamental belief in the orderly process of our political institutions. Camelot was shattered and with it, all its politically inspired romantic imagery vanished. Its portrayal of the neo-idealism of truthful and just government analyses and pronouncements, constitutional equality, merit-based advancement, and transparency of process all disappeared.

The gut-wrenching events of November 22, 1963, in Dallas's Dealey Plaza paralyzed the nation. It was a political and personal catastrophe. We lost our president.

Deeper, a fabric was rent that is yet to be mended and may never be. Shortly after the assassination, within weeks, FBI

Introduction ix

Photo 14-6. Frame Z 312. (Zapruder Film © The Sixth Floor Museum at Dealey Plaza)

Photo 14-7. Frame Z 313. Zapruder Film © The Sixth Floor Museum at Dealey Plaza

Director J. Edgar Hoover proclaimed that the alleged assassin, Lee Harvey Oswald, acted alone without foreign intervention. Case closed!

The government sought closure; the people demanded the truth. Portents of a winter of despair were about to dawn.

Over the years, the Kennedy assassination has receded into mythology and has become—like the tales of the Old West and the lives of secular saints such as Washington and Lincoln—fair game for the fabulist, the moralist, and the entertainer. Libraries have been filled with books offering vying theories: some have been in support of the WC, and some are indignantly opposed. All of them postulate with passionate certainty the righteousness of their cause. To be sure, some treatises rise to the level of admirable scholarship. The most outstanding and valuable of those are narrations by the authors who played a significant role in these historical events.

Renowned experts with acclaimed expertise in treating trauma victims attended to President Kennedy in the emergency room inside Parkland Memorial Hospital, just moments after the fatal bullets blasted through the president's head, causing his death. The Parkland trauma staff recount in vivid detail those tempestuous, spellbinding, percipient firsthand observations, analyses, and medical procedures undertaken to try to save Kennedy's life. They documented these events with a medical precision that memorialized an *evidentiary foundation*, revealing tracts of bullets' entries and exits passing into and out of Kennedy's body and the condition of Kennedy's head wounds.

The Parkland attendees inside trauma room 1 were important witnesses in the truth-finding process. Yet, some who offered emergency care to the president and whose observations were corroborated and memorialized in writings and diagrams were *never* called to give testimony to the WC.

Most notably, based upon expert findings, were conclusions that the fatal shot, seen at Zapruder frames 312 (Z312) and 313 (Z313),[1] which killed Kennedy, entered the president's head and body from the geographical right front (the stockade fence area) and not from the rear (the Texas School Book Depository building).

Expert testimony would have put into question the WC findings by contradicting its central theme that Oswald, the lone gunman, fired three shots at the president only from the rear as the motorcade passed the depository building.

This extraordinary WC omission and failure to chronicle the events of the assassination accurately appears in other relevant areas as well. In this way, the WC created a fog of deception that has substantially called into question its authenticity and credibility.

If the WC was engaged in a virtuous search for truth, then there is no rational reason to omit the Parkland experts. However, if the WC was a façade devoid of investigative legitimacy, designed to tailor its faux investigation to a predetermined conclusion, then those involved in meeting that goal readily accept the reality of its deception.

In early 1977, I served as deputy chief counsel to the Congressional Committee investigation into the assassination of President Kennedy. During the course of my probe, I came into possession of a memo dated November 23, 1963, from FBI Director J. Edgar Hoover to all Bureau supervisory personnel. It stated, *inter alia*, in substance, that the FBI agents who had questioned Lee Harvey Oswald for approximately seventeen hours immediately after Oswald's arrest had listened to a taped conversation between an

---

[1] In Dealey Plaza, Dallas, Abraham Zapruder was standing on the north side of Elm Street filming the presidential motorcade in which JFK sat upright in the limo. Zapruder's film provides 18.3 frames per second.

individual who identified himself as "Lee <u>Henry</u> Oswald"—a fake LHO and an individual in the Cuban Embassy. The conversation originated inside the Russian Embassy in Mexico City by this faux Oswald, who telephoned the Cuban Embassy. The call was made on or about October 1, 1963, just about seven weeks before the assassination. The Hoover memo noted that the agents who questioned the real Lee Harvey Oswald concluded categorically that the voice on the tape was not that of Lee Harvey Oswald. Based upon the evidence adduced during the investigation, I had reason to believe that David Phillips, the third-ranking member of the Central Intelligence Agency (CIA) in charge of Western Hemispheric operations, employed a *nom de guerre*, Maurice Bishop. Bishop had a significant involvement with anti-Castro Cubans and Lee Harvey Oswald.

I had Phillips subpoenaed to appear before the House Select Committee on Assassinations (HSCA) in executive session. I asked him under oath where we could locate the tape of the alleged Oswald conversation of October 1, 1963, while inside the Russian Embassy in Mexico City. Phillips stated that it was CIA policy at the time to recycle the tapes every six or seven days and it was no longer in existence after the first week in October 1963.

I then handed him the Hoover memo, which, according to the FBI director, clearly revealed that the tape was evidently available in Dallas on November 22 and 23, 1963. Phillips read the memo, then folded it, placed it in his jacket pocket, arose, and walked out of the hearing. Interestingly, Phillips had already been questioned by chief counsel Richard A. Sprague in late December 1976 and rendered the same answers re: the alleged present unavailability of the October 1, 1963 tape—it had been recycled! So stated the CIA! At that time, Sprague did not have the J. Edgar Hoover November 23, 1963 memo.

I immediately urged the Committee to recall Phillips and advise him to obtain legal counsel so that he could be given an opportunity to purge potential criminal charges of contempt and perjury. Also, there were many more questions that he needed to answer. I further advised the Committee of the urgency of the matter and gave them legal options. They chose to do nothing. Thereafter, our staff phones were denied long-distance telephone access, franking privileges (free mail service) were withdrawn, and staffers' pay was withheld.

Prior to my assignment with the Congressional Committee, I served as an assistant district attorney (ADA) in the New York County (Manhattan) District Attorney's Office (DAO) under legendary DA Frank S. Hogan. While there, I successfully prosecuted scores of felony and related murder cases to verdict. I was bureau chief of the criminal courts, ran the homicide bureau, and was in charge of the training program for the legal staff.

From experiences as a prosecutor, I knew well that there is no political way to investigate a case. There is no liberal or conservative way to gather evidence, and there is no Democrat or Republican way to evaluate it. Unfortunately, the Congressional Committee played politics with our investigation and subverted it. The members breached the trust reposed in them by the American people. They assured me that whatever the facts revealed would be forthrightly presented to the public. Regrettably, that was false.

Equally distressing, contrary to the credible facts, the WC made conclusive findings that on October 1, 1963, Lee Harvey Oswald made that telephone call "in Mexico City" from inside the Russian Embassy to the Cuban Embassy. It, too, breached its duty to engage in an unconditional effort to report historical truth. For many reasons, the WC investigation was fatally flawed.

The Parkland doctors, as well as other compelling evidence, present the case for shots fired from the front right of JFK, near the stockade fence, striking him above his right ear and blowing out the back of his head, all occurring while LHO was inside the Book Depository at the so-called sixth-floor sniper's nest, according to the WC investigation.

Lest we fail to understand the state of mind of the WC commissioners and investigators, I offer this classic, documented exchange between WC influential commissioner and former CIA Chief Allen Dulles and Chief Justice Earl Warren, of the US Supreme Court:

On or about the third week of January 1964, Waggoner Carr, the attorney general of Texas, Dallas DA Henry Wade, and Leon Jaworski, the chief counsel to Waggoner Carr, met on the record with Chief Justice Warren in executive session. They informed him that from an "unimpeachable source" (their description) Lee Harvey Oswald was a contract employee of both the CIA and the FBI. The chief justice responded with assurance that the information would be followed up with a fair inquiry.

"Not so fast," interjected Allen Dulles. The chief justice asked Dulles to explain. Dulles then stated in substance, "Well, if you ask J. Edgar Hoover if Oswald ever worked for the FBI, he will simply say no. After all, you know that he is already upset with us because he had early on concluded that Oswald was the lone gunman."

The chief justice inquired, "You mean that if I were to call an agent here as a witness under oath, he would lie?"

"If he were a good agent, yes," said Dulles.

"Then who will he tell the truth to?" asked the chief justice.

"Maybe the president," replied Dulles.

Sadly, the WC treated the matter just as it did with the Parkland doctors: it did nothing!

All told, the American people expected a straightforward, fact-finding foray leading to historical truth. Instead, it was given a Lewis Carroll *Through the Looking-Glass* fantasy form of due process: first the sentence, then the trial. And if the accused is thereafter found not guilty, *"'All the better!' says the Queen."*

PART ONE
CIRCLE OF TRUST

Facts are stubborn things, and whatever may be our wishes, our inclinations, or the dictates of our passion, they cannot alter the state of facts and evidence.
—John Adams, argument in Defense of the British Soldiers in the Boston Massacre Trials, December 1770

CHAPTER 1

I Know This Much Is True

Lee Harvey Oswald did not kill JFK.

Stick with me here. You've heard it said before and you may land anywhere from considering it the most understated "given" in American history or a fringe manifesto motto from voices who easily veer conspiratorialist.

But I am neither—not one who assumes nor one who mysterizes. Rather, I have a unique relationship with and to the truth—and to this case. I was at the center of it, tasked with the very responsibility of finding truth, and divinely tasked long before that in ways I wouldn't come to understand, until now, when the whole picture blends into focus, and of every word I've ever written, every book ever published, any case ever won, this is the one—above all—that perhaps matters most.

In pursuit of the truth, I offer no opinions, inclinations, wishes, or conspiracy theories, only those "stubborn things" called immutable facts which inexorably validate the search for truth.

That by itself would be enough, for truth is truth, no matter the bearer of it. But underpinning this delivery, you have to understand who I am, who I've worked with, who I trust, and the history (professional, personal, spiritual) that makes it impossible to turn a blind eye, stay quiet, or do anything less than blow the lid off this very weak house of mirrors and shadows.

I've spent my life in books, and all the many pages between jackets have a common thread of chasing justice in some form or another—fact or fiction. But this is a very unusual book for me. It's personal. It's powerful. It has to be said.

We're unpacking something infinitely consequential and in order for it to carry the merit it needs, you'll need all the groundwork—every layer of firm foundation I have to offer you. Let me tell you: those layers run deep!

So, what I've done here is present the findings as if I were trying the case in front of a jury. To receive those findings as refutable could be accomplished through basic fact-checking and personal research, were readers to have access to the files attached to what I've come here to deliver. In court, however, there are checks and balances, and the legitimacy of position—the lawyers and judges follow protocol and licensing, credited by their state bar. Here, outside of the courtroom, I offer you other deep testimonies of credibility:

1. I am a fanatic about *preparation* and my uncompromisable *search for truth*. My reputation for this precedes me in the legal community, but as a reader, I want to introduce you meticulously to where that comes from.

2. I am inseparable from a deeply ingrained *history of values*, rooted in honesty and justice, no matter what that means—even if it means exposing, enduring, or in some shocking and bold cases, walking away.
3. *I am not alone*: These values were born and grown in me—then borne into action—from the very start, with everyone who influenced me from childhood and forward. Most importantly, they were exemplified and doubled down for me by some mighty men of valor, as the saying goes: namely, Frank Hogan and Dick Sprague, but they're leading actors in a lengthy cast of supporting characters.
4. I am aware that every turn involved an unquestionably *divine degree of intervention*. From the things that led me to a specific university, which led me to an interview I should have never been able to get with Frank Hogan, to Rick Albrecht doing what you'll see he did, to doors that flung open, and pieces of the puzzle that came together later in life, like the final round in *Slumdog Millionaire* where every detail led to an uncanny knowledge of, or exposure to, the answers everyone was seeking.
5. I am not fighting only flesh and blood, but I'm determined to live out *a deal I made on high* to deal with the devil and spend my life fighting evil in all its forms, with every tool I've been given.

You put those together and you've got this incredible truth-seeking rainbow where I made this deal that would set the trajectory of the rest of my life.

While facts are facts, they're also easy to question, especially in today's culture when you don't know where to turn for a fact check you can trust. There's a difference between what seems like a cut-and-dried case from a legal team steeped in corruption, versus a clear case with evidence accounted for by someone you would trust with your life, and who you've seen make the hard choices in favor of honesty—even when honesty was not necessarily in their favor.

With that in mind, in order to present not just this case but, deeper than that, to do so on the firm foundation and the tested and tried history of the staunchly steadfast characters behind the evidence, this book is organized in three parts:

1. Who I am—the VALUES I can't escape and the VIRTUE I know I'm called to chase.
2. Who these TRUSTED PARTIES are and how that fraternity influences and blends with my fantastic search for truth, even when truth is stranger than fiction.
3. The IRREFUTABLE EVIDENCE to which I have rare and unusual access, the validity of which is firmly ensconced on the two foundations above.

I'm going to be repetitious as we go through this. But repetition brings CLARITY, CORROBORATION, and CONFIRMATION.

Clarity: The best professor I ever had at Berkeley told us the same thing in three different ways when he lectured. It's a tested and tried premise in teaching and speaking: Tell them what you're going to say, say it, then tell them what you just said. It's solid.

Corroboration: When you're testifying or questioning a suspect, depending on what side of the case you're on, consistency is a trusted tenet of truth. It's hard to remember the same lie, but the truth will always be the same story, never wavering, easily recalled.

Confirmation: When I try cases, I don't just build up to a point and move on. The jury has to remember what I said in the beginning, so you bang it home—time and time again, landing on the same facts, unable to avoid the truth, and validating beyond a reasonable doubt.

When we started this missive just a few pages back, I explained that I do this not as a conspiracist or even as a researcher or historian—legitimate voices, but still limited in their exposure, access, or intel. I do this from a rare vantage point at the center of the original investigation.

In late 1976, I was appointed deputy chief counsel in charge of the congressional investigation into the assassination of President Kennedy. Like every other step that led me to that pre-eminent position and opportunity for impact in such a significant turn of events, this was profoundly, divinely influenced. It was against odds. At first, it was even against my own choice.

Upon my appointment and during my initial meeting with members of the House Select Committee on Assassinations (HSCA), I suggested that the Committee NOT hire me. At best, I opined, Congress is well-served by compromise. I made it quite clear to the HSCA that in my view, in general terms and in ordinary course, one should not compromise during a search for truth. Committee members assured me that they would not interfere with the fact-finding probe.

That assurance was one of the prime components in my agreeing to go forward, but several months later, I would regrettably learn otherwise, which, without question or hesitation, necessitated my resignation.

Why would I walk away? Because staying would mean standing there in the shadow of a known and unquestionable truth, shrinking in the bright light of it, while putting on the cloak of corruption I'd watched too many wear—the straitjacket of coverup that I'd watched ruin too many lives, from Main Street to Wall Street, from private lives to household names, from innocent individuals to career criminals. I was incapable of standing in truth's shadow and not stepping into the light.

The HSCA, however, was NOT interested in searching for truth and not interested in discussing it further. It was a "conversation over" situation. Actually, I retract that statement—the conversation *wasn't* over at all. In fact, it was just beginning—beginning to be distorted magnificently through a complicated parade of smoke and mirrors. The Committee would ultimately fabricate a significant portion of its forensic medical panel summary report, and to protect this fabrication from being discovered or revealed, it sealed all the underlying documents—for fifty years.

Here's what happened.

* * *

It was customary for Congressman Lou Stokes, Committee Chairman, to meet with me weekly, when possible, to discuss the activity of the Committee's search for truth. Stokes had recently been elected to Congress. He hailed from Cleveland and was asked by his brother, Carl Stokes, the first Black Mayor of Cleveland, to participate in structuring a new congressional seat that would bring substantial federal dollars to the city designed for its betterment: schools, public education, infrastructures, police protection, and citywide economic revival.

Chairman Stokes was a highly respected criminal defense trial lawyer. We were the perfect pair to get along and do the nation's business—Stokes, the consummate legal eagle defense attorney, and I, the unrelenting, impactful prosecutor. In fact, we got along famously and became lifelong mutually respected colleagues and friends.

At the time of our meeting, I had concerns regarding the Committee's majority membership embrace of political interference with its search for truth.

Accordingly, I began my presentation discussing the troublesome facts that reflected negatively on the CIA and its potential involvement in the entire assassination process. I did this without false confidence, fully aware of what I might be stepping into (though still not expecting exactly the results I was about to encounter), as I recalled Pennsylvania Senator Richard Schweiker's admonition to me the first week I was on the job:

"Beware," he warned, "the CIA will stonewall your investigation, refuse to hand over key documents, and intentionally mislead to further advance its cover-up—all of which it has done monumentally already. You see," he went on, "during my participation in the Senate investigation regarding possible executive intel agency abuse, I came to realize that the God-awful truth was that the CIA participated actively in the assassination of our president."

It was as straightforward a declaration as one could make. He didn't falter.

He then handed me his case file on the matter.

* * *

What I carried in that case file—what I found in his work from the start, what I would cull together in my work on the case, and what I would ultimately present—was clear and irrefutable evidence, corroborated by major players from every different area of the investigation including medical, legal, forensic, etcetera.

When I carried my completed findings into Stokes's office, I was aware of the foreboding warnings I'd received, but I also assumed this evidence was too vast and too rock-solid to ignore. Sometimes the noise is loud enough that no amount of establishment or corruption can shut it down. Sometimes the cat just can't stay in the bag. I knew that was what I had. A loud and unavoidable, hard truth.

When I completed my briefing for Chairman Stokes, I requested that the HSCA authorize a series of subpoenas for the obvious purpose of continuing our search for truth. Lou looked down and shook his head, then raised it.

"Bob," he said with a bit of twang that was familiar in his voice, "what you've done here is admirable, to be sure, but I don't believe your request for subpoenas will be honored. I know that surprises you, given all the time you've put into the investigation. Your work has been professionally outstanding. But" he stated almost whimsically, "this is Washington, DC, where power is supreme, and confrontation and scandal are verboten. The investigation has clearly indicated that the CIA participated in the assassination. No way these HSCA Committee members are going to support you. Bottom line, they fear CIA retaliation."

"You mean that I no longer have the Committee's support?" I queried.

"That's right," Lou replied.

"Then why did you hire me?"

"Frankly, the Committee majority never thought you'd get to the bottom of the sordid mess."

I shook my head, staring at Stokes. Sounds of silence bounced off the walls of his office.

He broke the silence asking me simply what I intended to do.

Reply at the ready, I leaned forward and said to him, eye to eye and with surprising ease:

"Resign!"

* * *

The next several steps were clear and played through my mind before I said another word. I told him in the same breath that I would be conferring with Dick Sprague. I then rose from my club chair, gathered my note pads, and left.

As I was leaving his office, I paused at the door, turned to Lou, and asked, "I assume that the Committee's lack of support applies to Sprague as well?" Lou simply nodded affirmatively.

Back in my office, I placed my legal pads on my desk, teeming with outlines of our evidentiary cumulation, and called Sprague. It was a short conversation during which Dick emphatically endorsed my position. He was one of the columns of truth I'd come to see as holding up the very tenet of justice. I knew he would be both as disappointed and as unrelenting or unhesitating as I, to turn away from any hint of cover-up, no matter what that meant for either of us, past, present, or tenuous future.

So it was no surprise to me when he confirmed he also wanted to have a meeting with Stokes to submit his resignation and to tell Stokes his opinion of the Committee's pathetic collapse of the truth-finding process and its shameful violation of its official obligation to honestly, without fear or favor, report to the American people.

Safe to say, Dick Sprague was upset and disheartened—to put it mildly.

I arranged for the meeting with Chairman Lou Stokes in his office that evening, as Sprague requested.

As I sat there at my desk—the reality of the situation hitting me in full—I became lost in thought, spanning time.

How could this all happen? The investigation yielded critical immutable evidence that led inexorably to the conclusion that an unelected bureaucratic federal intel agency, the CIA, had marked involvement in the assassination of JFK.

First in my thoughts was the composition, the assemblage of the Warren Commission (WC). Allen Dulles, who lobbied his way on, and previously served as CIA Director, who JFK fired in 1961, was uppermost in those thoughts.

From the investigation, it became clear that the WC's purpose was to rubber stamp the findings of Hoover's FBI and Dulles's CIA, both with substantial embarrassing ties to LHO. For example, within hours of the assassination, Hoover issued a statement that the Dallas PD had captured the killer, "a nut from the pro-Castro crowd." Both the CIA and FBI managed the evidence to achieve the contrived predetermined "lone nut" LHO conclusion.

The power to control nourishes the corrupt players, in and out of government, to the extent that our institutions are under assault to resist the egomaniacal mindset. It's real and evil and constantly requires effective, forthright individuals who fearlessly seek truth.

I was fortunate to have had mentors whose <u>values</u> and selfless professionalism guided me throughout my life. Often, I've thought about how values, the rights and wrongs, influenced my own growth and conduct in my attempt to do simply the "right thing." Faced with the total collapse of HSCA's credibility, I only more deeply realized the impossibility of collapse within my own values, going all the way back to the origins of my chosen behavioral pattern.

Here I stood: Note pads full of crushing absolutes. An impending gavel of a meeting between a marvel of integrity and the seeming bastion of security and intelligence, where the two should-be bedfellows were bound to implode in insurmountable conflict. And me. I'd made a promise to stand against evil. I'd been called to this. Every turn in my life—lessons in Brooklyn boyhood, how character counts on competitive basketball courts, how corruption and due process coursed through the courthouses of New York City, and a promise I made to God in a ripping turn of heartbreak—had set me at this desk, discovering what I had, and walking away from it. I didn't know how or how long it would take, but I knew there would be a day when there would be a way to let the truth be known.

That day has come.

But there at my desk, I was stuck in a cyclone of what had come before and where to go from here.

CHAPTER 2

Right from the Very Start

A case is everything in its evidence. Facts are facts, or so they seem. "Evidence" is nothing if it isn't true. It's nothing, if you can't trust the one handing it to you. Whether it's handed over on a silver platter or silver bullet, what is truly everything is your circle of trust.

Mine had been forged in steel and stone since my childhood, flanked particularly by two names who not only loomed high in legal and political circles, but who would come to reign supreme in the influence of my career and my personal life.

Dick Sprague and Frank S. Hogan were groundbreakers and world shapers. These men stood on truth and wouldn't stand for anything less. For this, they were my heroes from the start. Granted, they are among a fraternity of like-minded giants—lawmakers and leaders who worked to cut a path in an overgrown jungle of corruption, control, misdirection, and misconduct, and who macheted a way for people like myself to follow that route and push further into unchartered territory of revelation.

To understand why I trusted them and their counsel with my life, you have to meet them as I did and see their influence woven into the fabric of right and wrong and radical truth, against all odds. You have to encounter them wearing the same backpack of values and honor that I was fortunate enough to be given at the time and in the way I was raised—the values and experiences that launched me into this path, equally as unable to turn a blind eye to injustice and seemingly destined to carry a torch of discovery and delivery.

These men had shaped me. My childhood shaped me. Loss shaped me and ultimately, my life's mission, as I promised God the loss wouldn't be misspent but would propel me into purpose. All of this—every moment of unlikely connection, empathy, second chances, open doors, and monoliths who had moved the needle of justice from small law offices to the highest courts and most elite agencies—circled around me in the moment I realized a cloak of secrecy was going to be pulled over the clearest evidence of the biggest "case" our nation would ever review. I was seeing the darkest diminishing of truth, and I had been influenced lifelong by some of Truth's greatest heralds. It encircled me like my world was spinning and I could see it all at once—from life lessons learned from my coach to knowing these men would stand with me on the grounds of truth and refusal to bend, I was stuck in a kind of reverie, and unfortunately, I knew what I had to do.

I knew, and there was no question. There was no hesitation. For many, it may have been a moment of indecision or struggle but when your mentors and jurisprudent forefathers are the likes of Hogan and Sprague—or with the Americana and ethics that teed me up through childhood, college, career—the mantle of responsibility when it comes to truth and justice becomes a stridently black and white garment. There's no gray in the wardrobe. There is right, wrong, and what you're going to do about it.

It's a given for me. But for anyone else to understand these absolutes, as well as how they prepared me to translate the evidence that presented itself after the Kennedy assassination, I'd have to turn the pages clear back to the beginning. It might seem like a trite turn to "once upon a time, I was born," but if it's not understood how the strings are tied from beginning to end, then it's not understood that if you pull one, the fortitude unravels. Without fortitude, none of it makes enough sense—why you walk away, or why you tell the story.

It was during my reverie in Stokes's office that all facets of "the why" played animatedly in my mind, scene by scene, like your life flashing between your eyes, but a life of events that not just influenced, but determined my thinking.

* * *

My father was a lawyer. NYU Law, undergraduate at Fordham, one of the largest Jesuit colleges in the world. But it was accessible because the tuition was negligible back in the day, and this was during the Depression. He became a member of the New York State Bar but would choose a business track for life due to the severity of the Depression. He had a high IQ and a very keen business sense, and he did very nicely from a middle-class point of view. There was never any wanting of anything in our family.

My brother Bill was three and a half years older than I, and back in Brooklyn in our shared bedroom, we competed in virtually everything we did as if it were the seventh game of the World Series: chess, checkers, cribbage, basketball, punch ball, and stickball. Life was competitive, interesting, always challenging, and fun. He has always been a caring, loving big brother who took everything in stride and impressively, never sweating his school exams, which he always aced. He was regarded by teachers and fellow students at PS 238 as the smartest kid in school and the best athlete, skipping eighth grade and being promoted from seventh in junior high into ninth for an early start to high school.

Beyond my brother, a good part of my daily life was spent with my dear friend, Victor Dubitsky, two years older than I. Vic lived in a neighboring building apartment. We played a lot of competitive sports, and though we were both living in Dodger-crazed Brooklyn, as total contrarians, we were diehard Yankee fans. My brother was the most dedicated Dodger fan imaginable.

Bigger than the ballfield, Vic's musical ability was outstanding. He had a magical ability to play piano by ear and sing ballads with amazing talent. He dominated every school play and was without question a gifted performer.

When it came to passion, however, far more than the performing arts, he wanted to play football at Lafayette High School in Brooklyn. Unfortunately, it wasn't going to happen. As brilliant musically as he was, he was not athletic. His turning point came when the opportunity arose to audition at the renowned High School of Performing Arts in New York City, the perfect place for him to nurture and enhance his greatest gifts.

Vic's father, Simon, was from the Old Country. He was an orthodox Jewish Russian who worked in scrap steel and metal works. He so proudly escorted his son to the Performing Arts audition and on the day of his acceptance, Vic told me how thrilled his mom, Rose, and dad were before dropping the bombshell that he'd decided he wasn't going to go.

I was truly stunned and asked him why? "Bobby, my man," he said, just the way he always did, "I'm going to go to Lafayette High School and play football."

"Vic," I pled, "don't miss this opportunity—it will change your life—you'll be a professional, you're enormously talented, everyone loves you, I love you—I beg you, go to Performing Arts." I promised, "I'll show up to see all your performances." Vic hugged me and said, "I love you too, big guy," but heartbreakingly, he never changed his mind and was cut from the football team after the early practices. Worse, he never went back to his true gift. He never played anything after that closure.

Oh, the sweetness and the sorrow—the former, the unabashed and widely appreciated expression of his enormous talent, the latter his life experience dimmed with a heavily weighted "coulda/shoulda" and the inevitable unbearable sorrow of missed opportunity.

He would later confide that he thought the musical gift would always be there as something he could come back to if he had to, but football was limited to the few high school years and a short window of younger years for any potential career.

From my vantage point, a front row seat watching the unfolding of a friend's choices, I came to understand more perfectly that the Gift we may receive from on high is one that merits respect and fierce commitment to engage and improve over time, understanding that the Gift is only "ours to borrow," and that it carries portent at its center and purpose in its wake.

You rarely realize, in the moment when you're learning something, that it will define who you become at the most pivotal points of your life, or will become the key to being able to accomplish what you are given in your lifetime to do. In hindsight, though, they're clear as day, and this was one for me. A front row seat to the equation of turning away from divine appointment or embracing what you've been given.

I didn't know it at the time, but I was being hardwired to notice and embrace that what is God-given might be imperative and is surely worthy of our effort and intention.

* * *

I was aware at a young age of the value of opportunity. The proximity of watching Vic's story may have been somewhat of a cue-ball, but there was also a general perspective of gratitude, and there was no shortage of reason to be grateful. Immutable evidence here, too. We were positioned in front of good options and striving to use those as tools to make strong, strategic decisions.

We moved in 1955 to New Rochelle, considered by many as a suburb of New York City. We'd lived in a nice neighborhood in Brooklyn comprising hard-working moms and dads struggling to clothe, feed, and keep a roof overhead. We moved when I was twelve years old and in the seventh grade—a time when things that shape you start to cement. This was at a time when the large estates in the area were being broken into lots, so my father was able to buy a three-bedroom home with a two-car garage with a garage room attached, full basement, two baths, other things we weren't used to growing up in Brooklyn. My brother and I each had our own room after sharing a room my whole life. There was light and space, room to think, and an opportunity to learn from the adults around me.

On Saturday nights, my mother and father would have their friends over. My mother was a gifted teacher and active in the teachers' union, and she was always concerned about politics interfering with good teachers, so tenure was a huge issue for discussion. My father's friends were active lawyers, mostly defense attorneys, and when they talked, they would invariably talk about

Frank Hogan's office as a tough office to beat because he only moved on cases where he had immutable evidence.

And I would listen. I was surrounded by a cadre of character, work ethic, and well-developed minds—and the insistence that the kids develop the same. It was essential to my parents that a solid public education for their kids would permit them to "aspirationally" choose the adult life they desired.

Another beauty of that move was the percentage of the population that played ball, which I was primarily interested in. Brooklyn was about 110 percent Jewish—there were about four gentiles at PS 238—so school games weren't the predominant focus. In New Rochelle, I found a new fit with the ball team there, which would set the stage for another influential pivot point where principle was fused by the influence of a good coach.

***

During the summer of 1957, I was fourteen years old and preparing to enter New Rochelle High School (NRHS) in the tenth grade, the beginning of the projected three-year high school experience that was standard in New Rochelle (junior high was seventh through ninth and the upper grades were ten through twelve).

There was a basketball league with the two city JHSs participating along with other b-ball clubs in the mix. I excelled early on, and was mentioned in the local daily newspaper, *The Standard Star*. Heady stuff for a teenager with a big ego. I had found out about a new basketball camp—Camp All America—organized and led by coaching legend Clair Bee and staffed by renowned Brooklyn school district coaches, the most notable of which was Lou Carneseca.

***

One note about connections at this camp and the lasting impressions from leaders and students:

Twenty years after this summer, I was a prosecuting assistant district attorney in New York County. At the time, I was trying a high-profile organized crime murder case. The Supreme Court trial part in which the case was assigned was packed during court hours. (New York felony trials take place in State Supreme Court, an equivalent of the Superior Courts in other jurisdictions—the highest court in New York is the Court of Appeals.)

One day when court had adjourned, I packed up my Redweld files and noticed that everyone had already departed except one person. While still in the well area of the courtroom, I watched this fellow walk right up to me. He reached out his hand and introduced himself.

"Hi Bob, I'm Mark Groothuis." We shook hands. I was more than a little surprised. Mark went on to say, "I've been following your career. I'm a lawyer in Queens and I have a gift for you." He handed me a book that was written during that wonderful 1957 summer at Clair Bee's camp.

I recalled being selected with several other campers to be photographed doing basketball skills as directed by Clair Bee himself for his *Make the Team in Basketball,* published by Grosset & Dunlap in 1961, the same publisher behind Bee's classic Chip Hilton Sports Story series. I had completely forgotten the entire matter once I left camp at summer's end.

I was stunned. Mark was regarded as the most outstanding "guard" basketball player in New York City. He attended Brooklyn Tech High School and was a great champion. How do I know? Mark was one of the camp players whom I had befriended. He was extremely accomplished and definitely a highly skilled athlete who taught me a lot.

In the courtroom we talked and reminisced for a long time. I so much respected not only his enormous talent, as he was truly gifted, but also his commitment to keep improving. Ultimately, my respect for him was grounded in his character. This, you'll notice, will be a recurring theme in a trusted cast of characters.

* * *

But back to camp in the summer of 1957:

I was looking forward to the opportunity to compete with the top high school players in the northeast, covering NYC and the surrounding metropolitan area, but after the first two weeks, I was miserable. My performance was pathetic. My shots were slammed into my head. I never even made it to the basket. So many defensive blocks where the ball struck me dead in the face, I just about had "Spalding" scrawled across my forehead.

To free myself from the humiliation, I called home and asked to leave camp. My parents promised to drive up to the N.Y. Military Academy site the next day and when they arrived, I climbed into the backseat and made up a litany of faux reasons for wanting to go home: the food was no good, camp was boring, the counselors were unfriendly. I had come up with a pretty hefty list. Should have tried my hand at the performing arts school.

With Mom in the passenger seat and Dad behind the wheel, there hung over my made-up list only the strange, awkward sound of silence. Both of my first-generation American parents had little interest in whether or not I played ball, but like most moms, mine was finely attuned to wanting her sons to be capable of living a responsible, worthwhile, meaningful life. She was the one who finally broke the ice, and in doing so, cut to the chase, turning in her seat to look directly at me before saying, "Is the real reason you want to leave that the boys at camp are better than you?"

Tanenbaum driving ball to basket.

Tanenbaum jump shooting from baseline.

Wow, no warming up in the ball pen! It was as though a lance pierced through my chest. Right on, Mom! For a few moments, I sat stunned. How pathetic am I? I tried to con my parents! To break the silence, and perhaps a little to redeem myself, I tried the truth instead. "Yes, that's the reason. I'm just not good."

Mom's response was basketball camp on the surface, but it was layers deep with "how to let your circumstances make you, not break you" as well as how to aim high, then aim higher, setting your sights above where you can see from where you stand.

She said, "It's not that you're no good. You're good, but you're only fourteen years old. You've enjoyed the adulation of success at the local level. Your mindset here should be to try and learn from the boys who are better than you and to know that you'll get better and better." Mom never broke her gaze as she went on. "Look," she said, "if you want to leave, we'll take you home and you could be a big fish in a small pond. But I don't think you want that. You always mention that you want to be Broadway not New Haven. Okay, enough," she said in her self-containing way, before challenging me to choose my path in life—not just "this one" but "this way." Choosing the way camp would go, or that all my roads would go—the way I would choose to live.

"What do you want to do?"

I made it clear that I would face the music, gut it out, man up. As my parents left the campsite and drove away, I headed back in, satisfied with my commitment to use the next six weeks as a major learning experience devoid of self-pity. That's when a strange thing occurred.

My camp counselor, Lou Carneseca, walked toward me and waved me over to him. When I greeted him with a big smile, he reminded me that we were to meet on the outdoor basketball courts over an hour ago. "Where were you?" he asked. I told him that my parents were just there and I laid out for him the reason for the visit, and the outcome. His response took me by surprise and became sense memory for how your circumstances can echo your tenacity and transparency.

"Well congratulations, Bobby, Scripture informs that the Truth will set us free." He told me that working together, he could teach me how to really play this game. "It's not going to be easy, there will be frustrations, but if you hang in there with me, in the end you'll play with the 'big timers' and more than just hold your own."

Upon reflection, I've considered my meeting Lou Carnesca right there in the camp's parking lot area, where I had just met with my parents, something more than just coincidence. I believe in "intervention." Good choices don't always equal good outcomes, but the result is far more likely when you set the table with truth and commitment, and more likely still when Divine Intervention and direction are involved.

For the next six weeks, we worked on my game. Technically.

Understanding and playing off the angles, slashing in rebounding, proper hardnosed defense and balanced pull-up jump shooting with my hands and arms fully extended, and always looking for the open man to take the lay-up.

The technique I learned on the court was all basketball at the time, but it would be clear in the years to come that I was learning the proper techniques of life and leadership.

Lou taught me beyond any doubt how to play aggressively with a winning mindset. Whether the opposing team played man-to-man, zone or boxing-one defense on me, Lou taught me how to navigate against it successfully:

With preparation, Lou constantly reminded me, winning becomes a habit in whatever competition I may choose to engage in.

Near camp's closing weeks, Lou arranged for me to play one-on-one in the gym against York Larese, regarded as the MVP of the NY All-City Basketball Team. Larese had just graduated high school and accepted a full ride scholarship to the University of North Carolina, the university that had just won the NCAA national basketball championship and held an enviable track record in any year.

Lou told me that Larese and I would play one-on-one from after dinner until early evening for a couple of hours each day and that he, Lou, would get me into my dorm room before lights out around ten.

Early on, Larese simply beat me every night. He was truly amazing. As time moved on, I would read the room, remembering Lou's coaching on technical skills and learning to implement them on instinct, and I kept making competitive improvement through these everyday practices. Preparation. Commitment. Shifting from thinking I didn't have the "talent" to instead learning to refine and implement skills that would make me realize I had ability that came solely from the work.

Finally, with camp season ending, it actually happened. As Lou had just entered the New York Military Academy gym, I hit the game winning shot. I leaped higher than ever before. Victory was so sweet, particularly against Larese. Champion that he was, he congratulated me with a warm smile and handshake. Lou went on to be the great St. Johns College coach and to this day, the St. Johns' basketball court bears his name.

I'd later realize that one winning game—it wasn't Larese I beat. It was myself. My old ways. Any threatening early habits of disbelief, self-doubt, limitation, or dismissal. I beat the "no," and realized "yes" was just a matter of doing the work, doing it right, doing it well. Then doing it again the next day.

* * *

The summer was the springboard by which I believed that I was ready to begin my high school experience. What I was actually walking into was far more than high school or any traditional teenage experience. It was clear that God was wiring me with what I'd need to get through difficult circumstances, not just surviving them but careening them into strengths and purposes that weren't defined before. During a season of extreme stress, an unsuspecting individual would come forward unrequested, to not only save the day, but to also encourage everlasting meaningful life.

* * *

At age forty-six, my mom contracted ovarian cancer. No one bothered to exactly explain what that meant, but it didn't take a PhD to figure it out. She had the required surgical procedure, which didn't curtail the persistent cancerous onslaught. Mom chose to remain at home during the so-called treatment period. Sadly, she had an extremely virulent deadly condition. As a result, she suffered enormously and her deterioration was rapid. Mom's younger sister, Aunt Barbie, moved in with us to help care for her on a daily basis.

Totally unbeknownst to me, the doctors forecasted to my father and aunt that Mom had just a few months to live. What I did know was that I was helpless to save or even aid my precious, dear mother.

As time went by, she experienced a temporary remission. I was now a senior in high school, and Dad wanted me to try to go about life as closely to normal as possible, concerned with what was passing me by—school and ballgames, not much else. To deal with Mom's pain, Aunt Barbie had asked me to administer morphine shots. The net result of my activity at home remained private. I told no one that Mom was dying. I was in total denial myself. "Mom will beat this monster predator pernicious disease! Just wait, you'll see!" I must have said all that and more to myself thousands of times to get through the day.

Near the end, Dad still wanted me to captain and lead my successful high school basketball team. When game nights were scheduled, I wouldn't leave Mom and Aunt Barbie alone until Dad came home.

That had been working pretty well, until it didn't. On one last game against our archrival with the championship on the line, I waited for Dad's arrival. Dad was late, got caught up with work. By the time he arrived and told me to get going, it was already 7:15 p.m. The game was scheduled to start at 7:00 p.m. I was never late, always got to the gym at least an hour early to shoot around and get mentally prepared.

My coach, Paul Ryan, had served as a hard-nosed drill instructor during his Army service. He coached a merit system. All that mattered was whether you could play and keep your mouth shut. He also coached football like a Vince Lombardi protégé. As such, he was honored as Coach of the Year in both basketball and football a number of times. We won the league several years in a row, with tonight's game pivotal.

When I got to the game, I ran into the gym, down the stairs to the locker room to change into my uniform and sneakers. My heart was in my throat. But something was unusual. When I hustled to the stairway leading to the locker room, I passed the basketball court that was filled with spectators but no play on the court. No action going on. Must have been a timeout.

I made it to the locker room, uniform on, sitting on the bench, I bent forward to try and tie my sneakers when my hands started shaking beyond my control. I stopped, brought my hands to my waist to pause, and tried again. Same result. Hands shaking too hard to tie my laces. But this time, as I leaned forward to get my hands under control, I noticed a pair of shoes in front of me. It was my coach. "Mr. Ryan" as we all called him. He looked at me without saying a word, kneeled down on one leg, and this hard core, hardnosed, drill instructor Army vet and legend of a coach, tied my sneakers.

I stood up. He grabbed me by my shoulders and said: "I know everything; your dad has called me to keep me informed."

Startled, I said, "What are you doing down here with the game upstairs?"

"No game going on," he replied. "I traded all our time outs waiting for you to get here."

Still standing there, Mr. Ryan declared like he was calling a crucial play, "You're going to make it through this ordeal, and be stronger and better capable to handle life." I just stood there staring at him. He shook me again. "Believe me," he said, "you're going to make it and lead an important life."

It wasn't just platitudes and encouragement, though they would have been powerful enough—it turned out to be a testimony, as he shared that he had endured similar tragedy. When he finished, he looked at me with understanding and we were tearfully deadlocked.

We hugged. We cried. We related. Then we went upstairs to take care of business!

* * *

These moments were character shapers, but the body of work from this time in my family's life—that was a mission maker. What would happen just around this bend in the road would become the reason that walked me into every office or courtroom, and the unexpected sense of divinity that propelled me. I would make a promise, then I would spend my life living to keep it.

* * *

Wondering how much worse things could get, I chose to recall often the special times I shared with Mom. We were theater buffs who would bond over Broadway legends and their showstoppers. Atop the list was Ethel Merman's *There's No Business Like Show Business*. She so captivated the audience. Critics claimed that regardless of where you sat in the theater, you could hear every word she belted out with thrilling gusto.

Mom and I could attest to that extraordinary professionalism and her mastery of theater acoustics considering Mom only had enough money for two seats in the last row in the balcony at five dollars apiece. Even in the nosebleeds, from the time the curtain went up, we were mesmerized!

We strived to see all the plays listed in the *New York Times* theater guide. We never quite made it.

We also shared a love for the great stars of film: Brando in *On the Waterfront*; William Holden in *Stalag 17*; Burt Lancaster, Monty Clift, Donna Reed, Deborah Kerr and, of course, Frank Sinatra in *From Here to Eternity*; and *The Best Years of Our Lives* with Frederich March, Myrna Loy, Dana Andrews, and Harold Russell.

These were larger-than-life escapes but even in the mundane, there was always so much more, from board and card games (gin rummy and canasta) to going over the current events of the day.

Then on the most painful morning, in homeroom at New Rochelle High, I received a note that our principal, Miss Loretta Coons, wanted to see me.

As I left the classroom, I saw my brother Bill, standing alongside Miss Coons. Nothing had to be said. I knew that Mom was now with the Lord.

It seemed like this season had been lifelong and sudden, all at once. Through all the hopes and devastations, the beauty and the ache, it was our last experience with one another that had left both of us speechless, and it had just happened the day before:

Coming home from school, I had closed the door and heard a thud, a noise like something had fallen. Mom heard me walking up the stairs to my room and called out to me—she screamed "Help!" I ran into her bedroom and saw her on the floor, tearfully telling me she had just fallen off the bed. I reassured her, "Ma, don't worry, I'll take care of you," and reached down to pick her up. With my mother now in my arms, I realized the savagery of this evilness. In my arms was this gracious, kind, hard-working, wonderful woman who was now reduced to a bag of bones. She was that light. Evil tore her apart.

I placed her back in her bed and with a kiss, I stayed by her bedside until she fell asleep.

That moment was a reverie of a different sort: I knew then, that even though evil had its own clock and wreaked havoc as it saw fit, I could harness and redirect the harm evil intended, into a sort of good. I would refuse to give it all that it came for. I would face off against this monster by making a difference with my life.

After the ordeal of the funeral, I began taking long walks alone trying to figure out how to process it all.

Then the insight happened with acute clarity. What was required was that I make a spiritual deal with the Almighty:

Provide for me evil, and I will bring it to justice, no special aid in so doing. I will always act in a righteous fashion. Notwithstanding evil's cruelty, I will force it to be accountable in due process oriented, court disciplined proceedings.

As I performed athletically, so will I similarly perform in the courts of law in a manner that will extend over the years to come—college, law school, and the courtroom—to prosecute the unjust. I will be prepared, and make it happen in due course.

This would become my mission, my identity, my calling card, my life. I believe I have remained faithful to it since the day it became clear. I believe I am continuing to fulfill that promise in the revelation of this book and the evidence within. Notwithstanding evil's cruelty, I will force it to be accountable. I will be prepared, and make it happen.

* * *

After high school graduation, an opportunity arose for me to meet the inimitable "Mr. Boston Celtic," team captain, the great Bob Cousy, who offered me a basketball counselor job at his summer camp Graylag in Pittsfield, New Hampshire.

I had submitted a letter to him requesting the job. It turned out that the designated b-ball counselors, of which there were six, were All Star college players. I explained to Cousy that I can handle the alleged All Stars but moreover, I wanted to learn from him. He responded by telephone and asked if I would meet with him for an interview. We did just that. He hired me for the eight-week job, but more importantly, we became lifelong friends.

We played every day, four-on-four halfcourt, "the Cooz" playing with a fervor to win every game. Cousy always made up the sides (teams) and would pit me against himself. Truly, I couldn't believe I was playing with the great one. He was amazing. The Celtics had just won the NBA World Championship. During the weekends, with the camper kids in attendance, we would play full court against the UConn summer team and other summer college teams.

"To my good friend Robert T with whom I shared many fond memories on the basketball court. Bob Cousy"

In this summer of 1960, I was seventeen years old, right out of high school. A "meant to be moment" was about to occur—another turning point and building block.

Pete Newell, who coached the University of California, Berkeley in 1959 to the NCAA national championship, visited the Cooz at camp during the summer, inquiring of Cooz who he would recommend in the Northeast to play at Cal. Unbeknownst to me, Cooz had recommended me. Pete Newell, a terrific coach, was then in pursuit but I wasn't set in my mind what to do and never responded positively. I did tell Newell that I was honored by his interest in me.

After the summer camp season ended, I played a lot of b-ball and felt great, but I had nowhere to go, when Aunt Barbie came to the rescue. She had called wanting to know what plans I had for continuing my education. I told her that I had no plans and didn't feel ready to continue on without purpose. She asked about the colleges that had recruited me and thought they would still be interested. Maybe, I responded, but I let everything lapse.

She told me that under no circumstances would she just sit back and watch me wither away. "You will always mourn Mom, but you have a life to live, and think how proud Mom would be to witness your maturation highlighted by your athletic gift which you know you must nurture."

In that regard, Aunt Barbie had contacted a school in DC, which she thought I'd like. "It's Columbian Preparatory. I'd like you to meet the Headmaster, Joe Debuque, a heavyweight in the Democratic Party in the western states." God Bless Aunt Barbie, a divinely driven person who cared about me and planned my return to the real world, beyond words and to the point of greatly effective action. She helped determine my future when circumstances seemed to be determining my demise.

A meeting turned into starting classes that fall in September 1960 in a one-year, post–high school term. There were about 150 students, most of whom were athletes destined for the Naval Academy and West Point. The purpose of the school was to allow the Athletic Departments of the Academies to obtain the required congressional appointments for the designated athletes attending Columbian Prep to be admitted to West Point and Annapolis and prepare them for the entrance exam.

When I realized what the school was about, it gave me a chance to have some fun and "nurture the gift," like Aunt Barbie had lovingly admonished. The gift that was "only ours to borrow" as I'd learned from my mother. The gift I'd learned from watching my childhood friend Vic, to not turn away from but to lean into and embrace.

* * *

Classes ran from 8 a.m. to 3 p.m. Afternoons were usually spent at the local DC, YMCA. At the "Y," I challenged all the scholarship players to games of one-on-one. To put it mildly, it was a real eye-opener.

Most of the players felt insulted and bragged how badly they were going to beat me. My attitude was quite different. I relished the competitive response to my challenge. After all the games, mostly the good nature of my opponents made it all a lot of fun. As athletes, we came together. The players voted me team captain and got ready for the games to be played against the colleges in DC.

During the season, the coach at Navy, Ben Carneval, who was an All-American at NYU, met with me. Coach Carneval offered to get me into Annapolis if I wanted to accept the appointment.

I would say it was crazy, but I was learning, it was all by design. There was a road being rolled out and all I had to do was keep walking. I did, but with a deep awareness that Aunt Barbie's intervention had to be spiritual—nothing less!

*　*　*

Once Pete Newell heard Coach Carneval offered me admission to the Naval Academy, he asked if I would visit Berkeley. I told him I would, but my mother just died, and I didn't want to leave my father alone. Coach Newell didn't waste any time confirming that my dad was encouraged to come along and that they would cover all expenses.

When we visited Berkeley, I was overwhelmed. It had everything I dreamed about going off to college: beautiful campus, top academics, and Pac 8 basketball. Dad and I spent the weekend touring San Francisco and Berkeley and just as we arrived home, I received a call from Howie Dallmar, the coach at Stanford. He said that he heard I just visited Berkeley. He assured me that no one picks Cal over Stanford. I responded that I had no idea about that rivalry but was certain that I'd be going to Cal.

His reply startled me. "Bob," he said, "I got you in on the Jewish quota!" I was surprised, to put it kindly. Never before had anyone so brazenly engaged me in an antisemitic moment. I'm not sure Coach Dallmar even understood what he had done, but it was a rude welcoming to the real world and I politely told him that I would not be visiting Stanford.

Cal won my vote for undergrad and for law school. Seven years went by in a flash and prepared me well for all the years I spent at the District Attorney's Office (DAO) in Manhattan under the leadership of legendary DA Frank S. Hogan—or for the day I walked into his offices to be interviewed as a third-year law student.

*　*　*

The interview almost didn't happen—or happened disastrously before yet another divine appointment directed me homeward and Hogan-ward, toward one of the most profound columns in the circle of trust that has encapsulated my life.

What I would begin to experience here, in large part, explains the earnestness and urgency of laying down the evidentiary findings of America's most mysteriously mishandled and misdirected case. It was all aligned and part of the same purpose that brought me through this case and here to these pages. From day one on campus, to day one interviewing in Hogan's office, my daily battle with evil was now begun in earnest.

PART TWO
THE TRUTH SHALL SET YOU FREE

CHAPTER 3

Higher Calling

I remind you: This was an interview that was in part made possible by the divine connections already forged in my life, not the least of which was my father's integrity and relationships in the legal community. I'd done the work and was coming in from a reputable law school having built a good reputation myself (from the b-ball courts to the mock courts, where character counts), but when it came to a firm of this caliber under the leadership and name of a guy like Hogan, I had no juice. No dog in this fight except the hand of God and my driving, ambitious desire to work for Hogan's team, no matter how much coffee I'd have to fetch, or proverbial water buckets I'd have to carry. I'd do the grunt work to be in good company with *great* work.

I was a third-year law student when I went in to start the interview process, the first of two interviews. I'd come in on holiday to get these done and this guy sitting behind his desk, the first interviewer, was a short, stubby guy who didn't seem too pleased to be doing this with his time.

I handed him a writing sample, which he flipped back to me with a "no big deal" gesture and said, "You know, we don't need any more John Waynes here."

Why not? I thought to myself. *He beats all the bad guys.*

Where did that come from? I knew I had something to offer and had always migrated toward leadership, but I was more hat in hand at this young stage, especially considering my impression of a legacy like Hogan.

So, I didn't say anything.

He asked me next, "Why do you want to be here?" I said, like any green kid in a major interview, "You know, it's just something I want to do for my life's work."

I went into "this ship has sailed" mode and just made it through until I left to go to my next interview, drastically deflated. I'm sitting in the hallway with my head in my hands, my elbows on my knees, thinking I am really up shit creek here because even if I ace my second interview with whoever's next, Hogan's not going to hire me after that fiasco.

I was literally grading myself, doing average-out math, thinking, *He's not going to hire an F and a D and an A+. So even if I got an A+ in the next-up conversation, I know I got a D/F out of this guy, and Hogan doesn't waste his time on C students or C players. I'm in an all-A's office here, and I have no plan B.*

I was up the creek without a paddle, as far as I was concerned, when I got a literal tap on the shoulder. I was so in my own head, I hadn't heard anyone coming.

This guy says to me, "Are you okay?" I was apparently right outside his office on the bench. I told him "No," because to me, there was no need to keep up the act of "prime candidate, start your bidding war." It was all over, so I thought, *Who cares if they see all my cards?*

As vulnerable as I was sitting there that night long ago with Coach tying my laces, here I was again on another bench, heart in my throat, in mercy's lap again. I might as well be 100 percent myself, because what the hell, I'm never going to work here, or for Hogan in my whole career.

So, when he said, "What do you mean?" I sold him my tell-all: "Well, I just had an interview that I got slammed to death on."

Now, this guy who's talking to me looked like Clark Kent. The whole get-up. The glasses, tall fellow, handsome guy in good shape. He seemed like he was someone to be reckoned with within the firm. Someone who might know a thing or two and who I could take at his word, so what he said next lifted my head and my spirits.

He said, "You're Bob Tanenbaum."

It didn't even seem like a question so much as a recognition. A statement. He seemed like he had all the answers in more ways than knowing who this kid was in the hallway.

"Yes," was all I could eke out.

He said, "You come with me."

So I did.

* * *

In order to have these interviews, you had to fill out various background information, so he already had a full file on me that had been provided. So he says to me, "I have all your material here, I get who you are, so just sit down and talk to me. Tell me what's going on with you. That guy you just talked to—I can't believe he pulled this stunt on you. How Hogan puts up with these people is beyond me. I'm leaving, so I'm not going to have to deal with this myself," he said, and it hit me: talk about timing. He was on his way out the door to become the leading lawyer in a major Connecticut law firm on matrimonial cases and family law—Rick Albrecht was his name—but here he was just in time to catch me in his net on his last days and keep me from fading out the door, dejected and separated from the people and purpose that would define the rest of my life.

"Put aside what this fellow just did with you, sit down, and just talk to me," he said.

Full reset; we were on our way.

*　*　*

"You know what I'm going to do?" he said after a bit. "I'm going to have you interviewed by another person."

While this was obviously encouraging to hear, I calculated it only on the level of getting back the interview opportunity I'd walked in with, nothing more. It was miracle enough to get back what I thought I'd lost. I wasn't prepared for what came next.

He called Hogan.

He picked up the phone (I thought to bring in a secondary interviewer) and said, "Ida?" Ida Delaney was Mr. Hogan's secretary, a very attractive young woman, well dressed. She was smart and confident, and she said, as unlikelihood continued to unfold, "Wait a minute, let me get him, he's here."

Albrecht said, "Thank you"—always very courteous, right down the line—and of course referred to him as Mr. Hogan, just like my high school basketball coach was always Mr. Ryan. Not Paul or anything like that. But these men, they earned this respect.

Men like Albrecht, too, took no nonsense about anything, because he said to Hogan, "Hello, Mr. Hogan. I have here a kid, he's terrific, and I want you to hire him."

I can hardly understand what's happening in front of me, but he goes on saying, "I know this is the only time and I know I've asked to get off this interview list because I've never met anyone I want to see hired, but this is an exception."

I'm listening to this. I can't believe any of this. With a little back and forth dialogue they're both saying at the same time that they want me to be re-interviewed by someone else and were trying to land on who, because Albrecht was leaving so they needed to find someone else.

But that's what was so wild about the divine timing of this whole exchange. Albrecht was leaving in two weeks for the firm in Connecticut. His family was very wealthy and owned seven or eight clothing stores in Manhattan. Earlier in his career, he decided he would leave Wall Street, where he was ensconced in a firm, to come to the DA's office on a traditional handshake commitment that, when you come in, you'll stay for four years. Hogan always said it took three years to really train people how to handle tough cases.

Albrecht was at the end of that stretch and about to be leaving in two weeks. In his office there were all these boxes he had packed up already. Here he was, just in time to catch me midstream and direct me right into a strong current that would carry me in the right direction.

Albrecht asked Hogan who he thought should step in as second interviewer, and Hogan said, "I've got the perfect guy. Mel Glass."

"Fabulous," Albrecht says, "Mel Glass is the right guy." Then to me he says, "You're in luck, kid. Mel Glass is very special around here. Go see him upstairs now," and sends me up, on a mission.

Frightening levels of coincidence were underfoot here that I wouldn't realize the full measure of until later years, but all these things are why I believe in intervention.

It was *that* Mel Glass who interviewed me on that twist-and-turn day that started with getting interviewed by the wrong guy—or who seemed so, but ended up being a divinely *right* guy because:

That failed interview led me to Albrecht . . .

who was leaving, boxes already packed, but still there just long enough to call Hogan . . .

who trusted Albrecht, and honored the pitch for a redux which led to me walking into Glass's office . . .

who was meeting with a couple detectives when I entered and who told me to sit down as they hastily left.

I was being moved through this chess board like a willing pawn, eventually to be blessed with king levels of mobility and ability. I didn't even know at the time what he had done. I'm across the country going to law school at Cal, falling backward into a situation I didn't half know the size of.

Mel says to me, "You have an interesting background here. You know what, I have an important question to ask you."

I'm just staring at him at this point. I don't know what to expect anymore, so my attitude is, "shoot, take your shots."

Apropos of that he said, "I see you played baseball and basketball in college. So here's my big question: Will you play here? We have an office team, Hogan's Hooligans, and we play all the highfalutin highbrow Wall Street law firms."

I said, "That'd be fun," and he said, "Good, good," with a big smile on his face. There was no pedantry with him at all. He was just a solid person who hated the media and the spotlight and would never give an interview. He had turned down $150,000 offered to him by *Life Magazine* to tell the story of the Janice Wylie and Emily Hoffert case at a time when he was making $18,000 a year. I started at $7,500.

But catch that—I started.

I'd been hired—in part to be a member of the firm's solid legal team, and in who knows how large a role, as a contributing factor to the other team, Hogan's Hooligans.

But I was hired, and that was my starting salary in August 1968. In September, we went to $9,000. And thereafter, we had another boost of $3,000. I was making $12,000 a year in short order, and I said to my wife, Patti, "This is amazing. We're getting $12,000, and if I were independently wealthy I'd have paid them to have this job."

It was the most fulfilling thing I'd ever done and, not to oversimplify, but it was also the most fun, partially because I had the room to keep trying in court, anything and everything. I had the world on a string, the greatest legal minds to learn from, and all of it would lead me to the greatest responsibility of investigating the JFK assassination later in my career, and later still—now—bringing those slam-dunk case files and findings straight to this page—something I do not do lightly, but also not with a moment's hesitation. This was always supposed to happen.

And I had come very close to not being hired at all, but Hogan would become like a father figure to me over time. People came to notice that. He sort of adopted me. He had no children. This was a man I would respect and follow quite literally to his deathbed.

For now, however, I need for the public to know why I would so want to work for Frank Hogan—not ambition or opportunity but who he was. Same as with all the others, Hogan at the top of the heap, but the whole cast of characters and their mettle matters. Their heart and tenacity, their values and mine. How those values became non-negotiable and insurmountable—key tenets in proving why these men (and myself) are only able to go about their work in the justice system in one singular way.

CHAPTER 4

Best Case Scenario: Trusting Frank S. Hogan

In case of emergency, break Glass.

Mel Glass was a guy who never faltered, even when confronted with a serious crisis. One such crisis began in 1963 when two young women, Janice Wylie and Emily Hoffert, were raped and murdered in their third floor apartment in the so-called fashionable Upper East Side of Manhattan. These brutal killings were highly visible cases that the media sunk its teeth into and dubbed the Career Girls Murders. It was in this hot spotlight of national attention, with pressure on to solve the case quickly and provide closure for the community, that an innocent young man, George Whitmore, was wrongly indicted for these heinous crimes.

I emphasize "wrongly indicted," though that goes without saying as the only definition of an innocent person being found guilty.

Then-ADA Mel Glass did not believe the evidence justified Whitmore's indictment—on the contrary, it exonerated him. When Glass showed Mr. Hogan this faulty evidence, Hogan summoned his bureau chiefs and asked Glass to "tell them what you just told me."

Mel did just that, and when Hogan asked these senior staffers what they thought, they all agreed they should cover up that Whitmore was unjustly accused. They urged Hogan to let Whitmore plead guilty to the murders—two murders he didn't commit. Doing anything else, they said, would put his career in jeopardy and vitiate relative case credibility, rendering confessions in other cases illegitimate.

On one side was an innocent life; on the other side was a single domino that could topple every piece of the justice system and turn the attention of devouring giants toward Hogan, stirring confrontations that could obliterate his reputation were he not to play along and turn a blind eye.

Hogan knew two things: This would convict a man who was not guilty, and it would leave the real murderer out there, wandering around the community, sure to kill again. He was appalled that it would even be entertained.

"You're asking me to take a plea from an innocent man, all because you're trying to save my career by covering up this mess?!"

They nodded affirmatively, sounding off, "Yes."

The pause was like a battleship starting to make a total U-Turn in still water. Engines down, direction shift. Hogan wasn't shy when it came to dealing with the justice system. He was sincere, and you can't get more sincere than what he did next.

Hogan slammed his fist on the desk, arose, and said with gravity, "What really torments me now is, I want to know, *when did we become so corrupt?*"

To Hogan, there was no option. He sent Mel downstairs to court to dismiss the false case against George Whitmore and get the ball rolling in reverse. In doing the apolitical right thing, not only did he not lose credibility, his legend soared.

It was a historic stance on a historic case. I covered all of this—the case, discovery, the manhunt that led to the real killer, Ricky Robles, the miscarriages of justice—in my first insider's account, *Echoes of My Soul.* But the case itself changed everything, and I do mean everything. This was the case that led to the creation and implementation of Miranda Rights. Hogan's tough stand would go on to permanently reform the justice system as a whole.

All it took was Frank S. Hogan and his Ministry of Justice.

* * *

To give you a little background on Hogan, it helps to give you a better picture of the chronology.

In 1935, Tom Dewey ("Mr. Republican") was appointed a special prosecutor to deal with the mountain of corruption in the justice system in New York.

Frank Hogan was a Wall Street lawyer in a small firm. He wanted to work with Dewey and Dewey hired him. Reminds me of me, wanting to work with Hogan. Everyone has their lead.

In 1939, Dewey moved up from special prosecutor to district attorney. In 1941, when he became governor, Hogan took over as DA in 1942 and held that office for thirty-two years.

Hogan became a legendary DA and made his bones overseeing a lot of the organized crime prosecution, which was running rampant at the time. Respect for him was impeccable. Public record

Photo by Sam Falk. July 23, 1967 *New York Times Magazine* "'Hogan's Office' Is A Kind Of Ministry Of Justice."

was imperative to him as he fought corruption against great odds, sometimes alone. He always said, "You give me the evidence and I'll convict, but don't just sit around and make noise about it. Show me the evidence, and that'll move the needle." Black and white. Wherever there was proof, there was no power or enemy he wouldn't face with conviction.

That's what happened when senior staff gathered in his office that day. Long-term industry veterans, and actual Vets, as many of these guys were post-World War II guys, hard chargers. But they knew—or rather, they learned—what their limits were with Hogan. If you don't have *immutable evidence* in these cases, *with corroboration*, you're not going to try these goddamn cases.

Hogan not only made it right, he also made a way. Time and time again, it would be he who broke through doors that enabled me to do what I knew I had to do with my life's work and deal with the promise I made from on high.

During my time in the DA's office, I never lost a felony case. Still, I couldn't have imagined how this was going to escalate over time and how the same sense of personal conviction—Hogan's, or now, mine—would later come in to play on an international scale.

Destiny. All of it. Destiny.

CHAPTER 5

Another One for the Books: Trusting Richard Sprague

It was another "major headlines" case that tied me to Dick Sprague, the guy who became staff director and chair of the House Select Committee on Assassinations (HSCA), which covered the assassinations of JFK and MLK. Sprague tapped Bob Lehner to do Martin Luther King (Lehner was with me in Hogan's office) and put me on Kennedy.

But the original case that tells you the whole story about Richard Sprague's character was this one, adding him to my fraternity of mentors and becoming the book *Coal Country Killing*.

Sprague was chief assistant DA in the Philadelphia DA's office when this case went down. When I tell you Sprague was brilliant, I don't throw those terms around, and he set his sights on the crooked bastion of power, "Tough Tony Boyle," who thought he

"To Robert—a great friend and a wonderful human being—with utmost fondness and admiration, Dick."

was above reproach when he decided to "eliminate the competition." He wasn't, thanks to Sprague.

In 1969, Tony Boyle had a couple of his union buddies hire three people to kill Joseph "Jock" Yablonski, who had also been in the union with him for about thirty years.

The union—the United Mine Workers of America (UMWA)—was the largest of its kind at the time and Boyle was corrupt. Fearing exposure, repercussions, and loss of power, he put an open-hit contract out on Yablonski.

Here's what happened and how Sprague stopped everything. It wasn't easy, because there were some major players involved, high political positions, and a lot—a lot—of money. You needed to be tough in order to deal with this, and I mean tough in the real sense of it, not just a little thick skinned.

On December 31, 1969, at 1:00 a.m., three shooters entered Yablonski's home. They killed his wife, Margaret, his twenty-five-year-old daughter, Charlotte, and him. The bodies weren't found until January 5th, 1970.

Meanwhile, in March 1970, Sprague becomes the special prosecutor from Philadelphia. This case happened in coal country, in Appalachia, and it was who Sprague was as a person that made him the perfect fit for what ended up being needed there.

Being patient and doing due diligence without fear and with great honor, Sprague was able to turn people in his favor. These people were knee-deep in Appalachian culture, which at first seemed to make them an impenetrable wall to outsiders, but respecting the so-called notion of "hillbillyism," he turned the whole bunch of them around toward truth, and that would make the case for him.

The shooters themselves were Paul Gilly, Claude Vealey, and "Buddy" Martin, but nobody could get to the heart of the corruption, Boyle. Sprague did incredible investigative work and made the whole house of cards come tumbling down.

It was a long and complicated road that led to Boyle's first conviction and a reversal in retrial, but by this point, Sprague and I were in Washington together and he asked me to try this case. He went through everything with me, and I said to him, "I'll sit in court with you if you want, but this is between you and Boyle. You must convict him yourself." He agreed to see it through, and the trial was in November 1978, but we were building trust through this whole thing.

Here's where Sprague's personality and trustworthiness became the biggest influence. Boyle had come up with an idea to "launder" the blood money to the killers through a fake initiative called the Research and Information (R&I) Committee. He claimed the union did not pay twenty-three retirees what they were due and now they had to get the money to them. But he recruited these God-fearing people of Appalachia to get behind this scam because of the close-knit loyalty in that community. "The union is the only institution or entity that ever cared about us," they thought. "We owe everything to the union."

Sprague recognized that was the mindset and took a risky approach: he indicted them. He didn't try them, but he indicted them, and it bothered the hell out of them. They couldn't sleep at night knowing that they lied, and that it was going to be revealed, and they slowly started to come forward. Sprague kept enough pressure on them, and he had a wonderful FBI agent, Bill Curtis, who really followed Sprague's instructions and was so patient with these twenty-three that they all came around and testified, and of course that changed everything with the case.

Sprague said, "No one takes a plea in this case; anyone wants a plea they plead to the top count." And that's how he saved all of these twenty-three seniors forced into this fake committee scam over this blood money (everybody thought they were being paid for their back work, which of course they never were, so it was a double whammy of trying to silence witnesses and swindling seniors).

They were plenty scared by the indictment, but what really scared them was the notion that, "God knows we lied," and in the Appalachian culture, character was king.

PART THREE
TRUTH BE TOLD

CHAPTER 6

Entering into Evidence

We opened this book in the middle of my briefing with Chairman Stokes on our "immutable" findings on the assassination case. We've gone back through history that proved the character of all the major players behind this investigation.

Now we return to the evidence itself. The smoking . . . guns. (Take note: That's not a typo, that word is intentionally plural.) But I'm getting ahead of myself. Let's open this case file (after all these years) and you can review the evidence with your own eyes.

THE SINGLE BULLET THEORY

For the past sixty years, the government's contrived case—that a sole gunman fired three shots from the sixth-floor sniper's nest window inside the Dallas Book Depository building—rested substantially on the alleged science offered to prove the so-called "Single Bullet Theory," and the alleged palm print that Lee

Harvey Oswald supposedly left on the alleged murder weapon, the Mannlicher Carcano rifle.

Let's analyze these contrivances—the so-called Pretense Probe:

What is the **Single Bullet Theory**? It is the shot heard 'round the world and echoed through time and eternity, and every public-facing report:

> *According to the theory, JFK was shot twice in the back. One bullet struck the back of his head, and another bullet struck his back approximately 5¾ inches below the neckline between a 22.5-degree and a 17-degree declination, establishing a downward tract.*

That seems forensically solid, reading it as a layman—or from a teleprompter—until it comes up against the pesky inconvenience of math and science. When paired with the rest of the evidence, it comes up sorely lacking in logic or accuracy because *that* bullet, were it one, to satisfy that Published Theory, would then have to somehow move upward 11 degrees in JFK's body, in violation of basic science and common sense, and exit JFK's throat.

But we're not done.

The Theory also has it that the bullet then struck Governor Connally in the right shoulder, striking his rib, and shattering his right wrist, and severing a tendon in his right thumb, finally landing on Governor Connally's left thigh. Yet, the so-called Magic Bullet remains in its pristine condition, throughout.

All of this mayhem and misdirection, according to **The Single Bullet Theory,** occurs while JFK sat upright in the limo throughout the entire **Magic Bullet** pretense probe. Remember, the only time that JFK stopped sitting upright was after the fourth shot,

Entering into Evidence 63

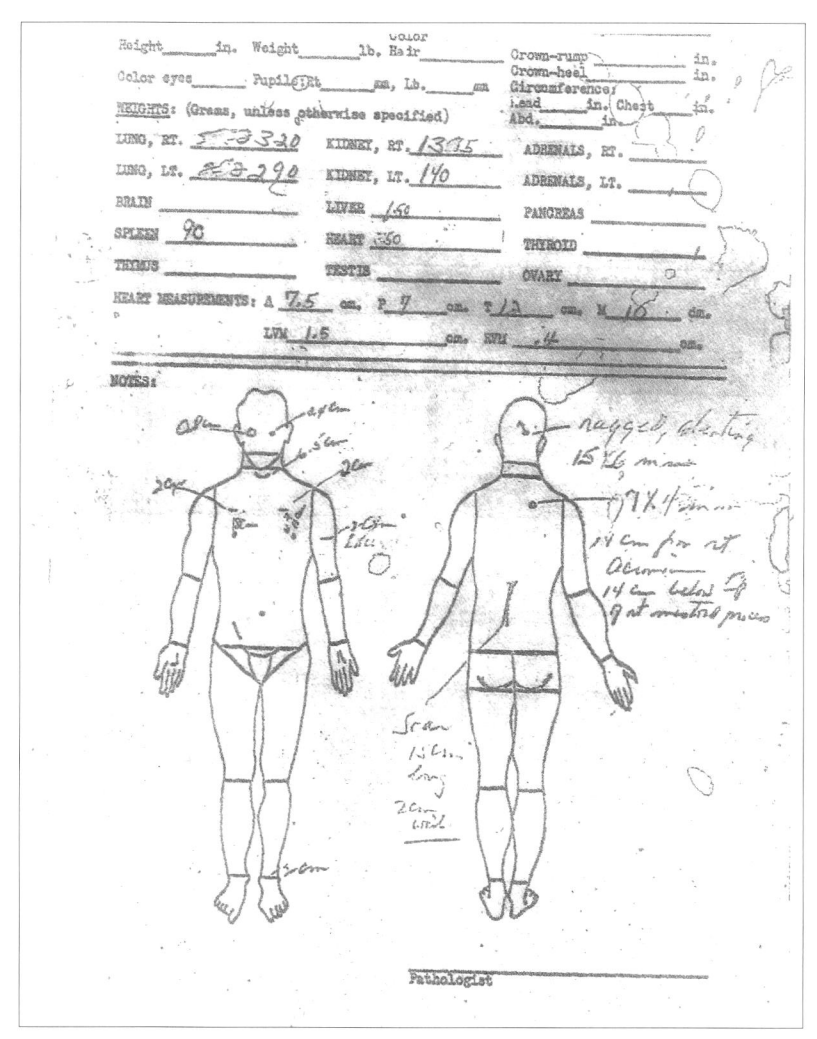

Autopsy illustration of front and back wounds to JFK. (Source: US Government Archive)

the impact of which caused his head to snap violently to his left and backward.

The **Single Bullet Theory** fractures credibility to any degree of trustworthy evidence.

THE MAGIC BULLET

As a further example, let's take a look at the **Magic Bullet** CE 399 itself.

In the government exhibit, it shows five bullets that the government test-fired and what the effects should have been on the Magic Bullet. In the exhibit, the **Magic Bullet** #1 is in supremely pristine condition. Bullets that were denoted #2 and #3 and which were shot into cotton wadding, expectantly show no damage. Bullet #4 in the exhibit was shot into a goat's rib and shows some deformity. But bullet #5 in the exhibit was shot into a cadaver's wrist and fractured its radius. As a result, it shows enormous deformity.

Yet, the pristine bullet CE 399 had allegedly struck Connally's rib . . .

and fractured his wrist . . .

but still remains in its pristine condition.

Thus the reason the CIA refers to CE 399 as the **Magic Bullet**.

It's an intelligence-insulting degree of gaslighting and sarcasm to say with a straight face or in a straight case, "This bullet hit bone repeatedly, which our forensics confirms would show 'enormous deformity,' but remained somehow pristine in untouched condition, and that bullet is your culprit." Now may I turn your attention to this bridge for sale . . .

To "convince" (read: intentionally mislead) the world of the accuracy of its findings, the government relied on a "scientific analysis" that allegedly verified the Single Bullet Theory.

NEUTRON ACTIVATION ANALYSIS (NAA)

The Neutron Activation Analysis (NAA) was offered as the principal testing component for Comparative Bullet Lead Analysis (CBLA). It was used to confirm that the bullet fragments in Governor Connally's right wrist matched the virtually pristine

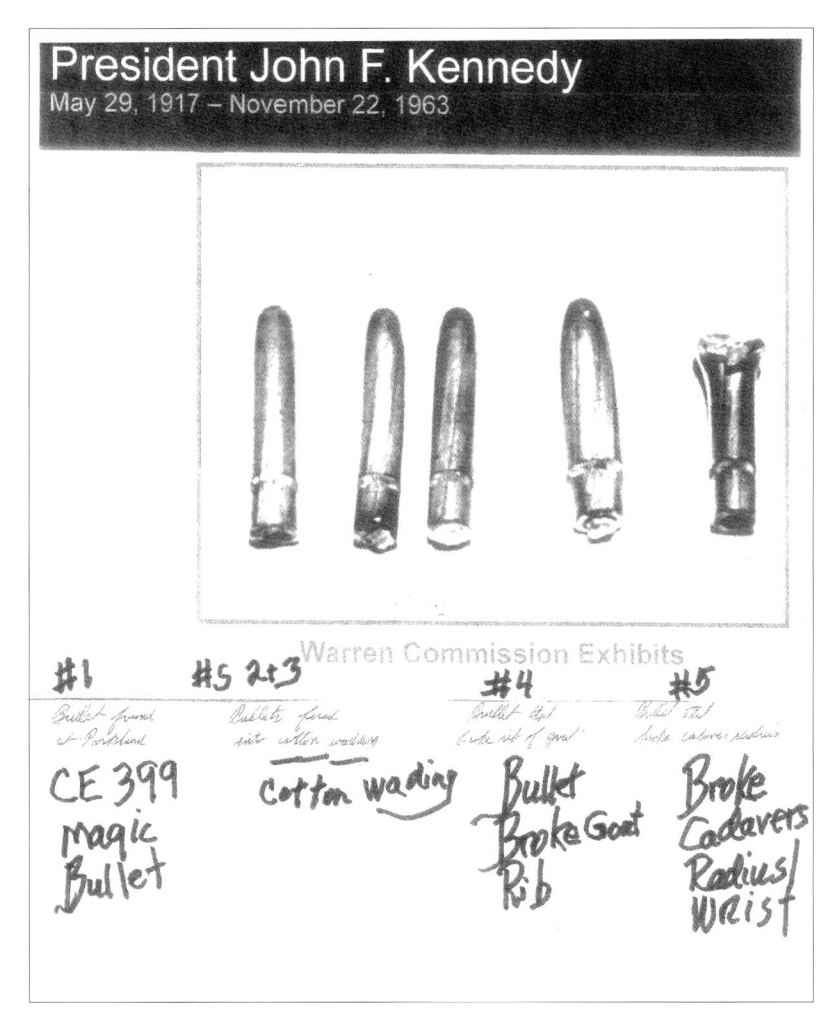

President John F. Kennedy
May 29, 1917 – November 22, 1963

Warren Commission Exhibits

#1 — Bullet found at Parkland — CE 399 magic Bullet

#5 2+3 — Bullets fired into cotton wadding — cotton wading

#4 — Bullet that broke rib of goat — Bullet Broke Goat Rib

#5 — Bullet that broke cadaver radius — Broke Cadavers Radius/WRIST

(Source: US Government Archive)

whole magic bullet, CE 399, and some of JFK's skull fragments matched the large fragments found in the presidential limo. Therefore, the argument establishes that only two pieces of ballistic evidence exist in the case, and both were fired from the alleged murder weapon, the Mannlicher Carcano, LHO's rifle. QED. Match, set, point, they claimed. Look over here in my left hand, is this your card? Which cup is the bullet under?

From 2002 through 2007, devastating critiques of the alleged legitimacy of NAA/CBLA were published in highly respected, peer reviewed, scientific journals:

- In 2002, Dr. Eric Randich, who holds his PhD in Metallurgy, published with several coauthors in the *Forensic Science International* journal, a comprehensive scientific analysis challenging the validity of CBLA and its principal testing component, NAA.
- In 2004, the National Research Council of the National Academy of Sciences published the research report, "Weighing Bullet Lead Evidence" that further impugned the validity of NAA/CBLA findings.
- On February 11, 2004, these findings were published in the *Chicago Tribune* entitled "Study Shoots Holes in Bullet Analysis by FBI" (which relied on NAA testing). In consequence of the findings made by the National Academy of Sciences, with FBI credibility at issue, the FBI turned to the National Academy of Sciences, which in turn asked the National Research Council to assemble a committee of experts to evaluate the efficacy and legitimacy of the aforementioned "CBLA and its principal testing component, NAA." The resulting study confirmed the critiques that NAA/CBLA were invalid and not to be relied on. Simply, you cannot match a fragment to a whole bullet or a fragment to a fragment.
- Accordingly, on September 1, 2005, the FBI shut down its metallurgic NAA/CBLA lab—the only one in the country at the time—and prohibited FBI agents from testifying about NAA/CBLA ever again because it had been proven that these attempts at forensics were unverifiable and frankly, debunked.

But who was paying attention when all this was reported? It wasn't exactly the leading news story. This was a pile of evidence to the contrary of the FBI's published findings—but it was a pile you only gained if you did the research yourself. Mainstream America was not spending its dinner hour researching truth and validity, and the story was barely being told.

The story was also just beginning. The magic bullet was just a small thread. The real magic is what happens when you start to pull that thread. The whole damn thing unravels like a bad sweater.

THE PALM PRINT

A few minutes after discovery of the rifle in the Book Depository on the sixth floor, Lt. J. C. Day of the Dallas P.D. examined it with a magnifying glass and later applied fingerprint powder to the side of the metal housing near the trigger. He noticed two latent prints and protected them with cellophane. Lt. Day also allegedly "lifted a palm print during the evening of November 22, 1963" that would be pertinent to the case, but let's verify this palm print and securing it into evidence.

Lt. Day apparently didn't photograph the palm print, protect it, or mention it to anyone and didn't give it to the FBI, which would have been required by protocol,

At 11:45 p.m. on Friday, November 22, 1963, FBI agent Vincent Drain picked up the evidence from Lt. Day, which at the time had no palm print, and brought it to the FBI lab in DC. There the rifle was analyzed by FBI expert Sebastian Latona, who claimed after inspection that the two latent prints protected with cellophane wrapping were of no value. Further, there was no evidence collected from the rest of the rifle that was processed for prints.

Read that sentence again. There was "no further processing of the rest of the rifle for prints" in the case of the assassination of a US president. Moving on.

He also stated that there was no trace whatsoever of a print (palm or otherwise) or of a lifting of a print. We'll read that sentence again, too: No trace of prints or of the trace of any lifting having been done.

It was Lt. Day's testimony that the reason he took photos of and protected the two latent prints (determined no value) but not of the palm at 8:00 p.m. on Friday evening, November 22, 1963, was because he was ordered by Chief Jesse Curry, Dallas P.D. *"to go no further with the processing."* But in an FBI interview, (CE3145) Lt. Day said that he received those orders from Chief Curry shortly before midnight; therefore, Lt. Day would have had about four hours to complete the processing of prints, i.e., photographing the alleged palm print, protecting it with cellophane, delivering it to FBI agent Vincent Drain with the other ballistic evidence which Lt. Day knew was being taken for analysis to the FBI lab in DC.

Remember that when Lt. Day handed the rifle and all other evidence to FBI agent Vincent Drain and mentioned the latent prints, he, Day, said nothing to Drain regarding a palm print.

On April 22, 1964, Lt. Day testified before the WC that he was unable to make a firm ID of the print during the time that it was in his possession. If so, then upon what evidentiary basis did Dallas DA Henry Wade rely on to publicly state on Sunday evening, November 24, 1963, that Oswald's prints were on the murder weapon? Further adding to the questionable existence of this palm print.

If that's a little hard to follow, it gets worse, and this one is easy.

Dallas Chief Jesse Curry, late in the morning on Saturday, November 23, 1963, told NBC in an interview that the partial prints found on the rifle could NOT be identified as Oswald's! On Sunday, November 24, 1963, the rifle was returned to Dallas Police. LHO's body was taken to Miller's Funeral Home in Fort Worth to be prepared for burial.

FBI agents dispatched to the Miller Funeral Home were armed with cameras, a crime lab kit, and the rifle. Paul Groody, the funeral director, noted that the FBI agents "stayed a long time in the Morgue. They put black gook on Oswald's fingers—which led me to believe that they did take prints of his palms." But why, because as reported in the *Fort Worth Press* on Monday, November 25, LHO had already been fingerprinted three times while in custody on Friday, November 22, 1963.

Finally, on Sunday, November 24, FBI agent Richard Harrison drove to the Fort Worth Funeral Home with two other FBI agents with the aforementioned print paraphernalia. The purpose, he admitted, was to obtain a palm print from LHO on the rifle that night.

But only for comparison with the *Real Print*, of course.

After Lt. Day's WC testimony, Day was re-interviewed by the FBI where he stated that he must have told Chief Jesse Curry that he (Day) had obtained the palm print in the evening of November 22, 1963. Yet, Curry, as previously stated above, indicated that on Saturday, November 23, 1963, he had already told NBC reporters that he had no identifiable prints in the case! Subsequently, Day refused the FBI request that he sign an affidavit swearing that he had in fact found the palm print.

We could set the whole print process aside as extemporaneous double-down evidence, because while it's corroborative, this case would already be on its head without prints. Too many angles. Too many bullets needed. The evidentiary bullet clearly unused. Ballistics widely and wildly refuted. The immaculate assassination.

As already discussed in detail above, the immutable evidence established overwhelmingly that the **Single Bullet Theory** was scientifically invalid and unworthy of belief. Because the validity of the Warren Commission's finding that LHO was the sole assassin rested firmly on the credibility of the Single Bullet Theory, and with that so easily debunked, scathing critiques were beginning to emerge.

Ballistics debunked.

Palm print deflated.

Yet, the WC and its advocates press on.

FORENSIC REENACTMENT

Zapruder's film shows Kennedy's head moving backward after being hit. The WC believed that was still consistent with being shot from the back. From alleged experts, it argued that nerve damage from a bullet entering JFK's head could have caused his back muscles to tighten and could have caused his head to move backward. Nowhere throughout all that's been analyzed has the WC and its absolutists ever mentioned the fourth and fifth shots and the enormous impacts that resulted, or what that means according to forensics. Or basic physics.

Nevertheless, without stopping, the WC determined to support its position by arranging for the following exercise. For the demonstration, it created ten gelatinized skeletal skulls modeled on human skeletal structure to be shot by rifle the same height and distance as LHO allegedly enacted.

Indeed, all ten skeletal heads were shot.

Contrary to WC hopefuls, all ten heads moved forward, not backward. Big surprise.

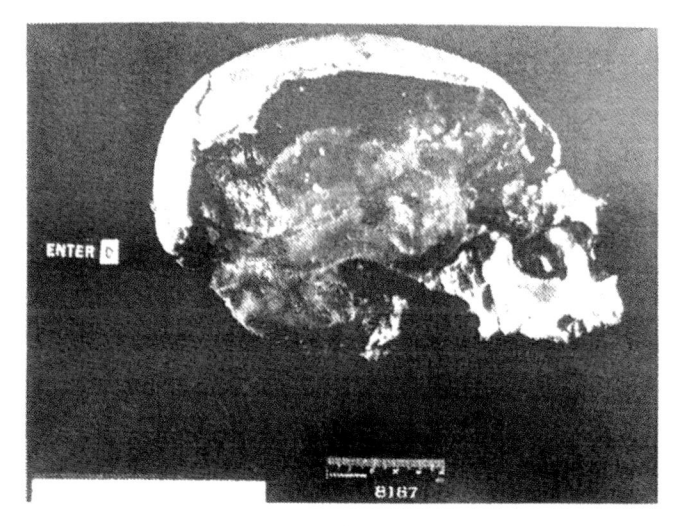

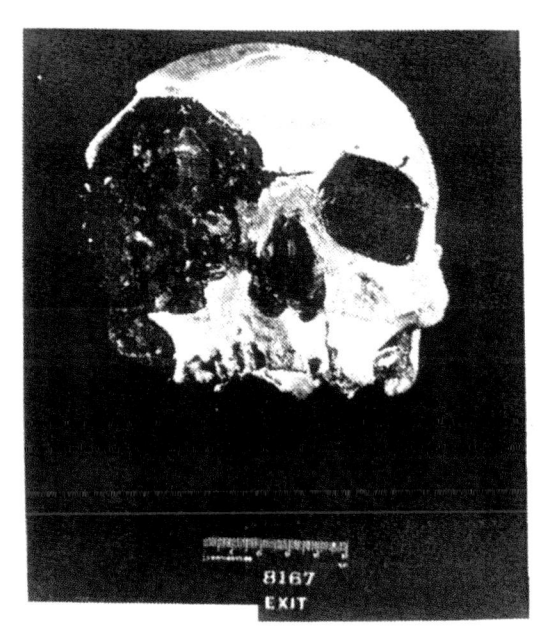

Figures 1 and 2. Warren Commission Exhibits 861 and 862 – photographs from "duplication" skull-shooting tests conducted at Edgewood Arsenal in 1964. (Source: US Government Archive)

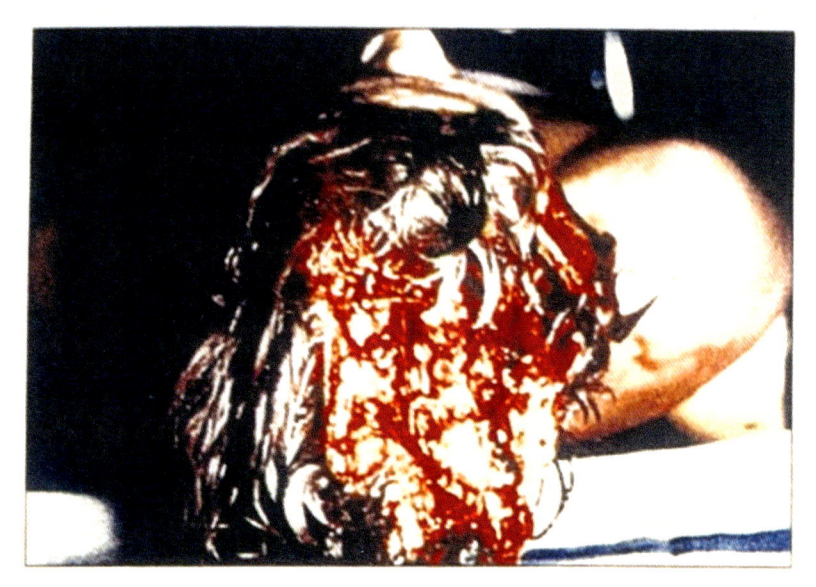

Photo 15-15. Autopsy photo of President Kennedy.

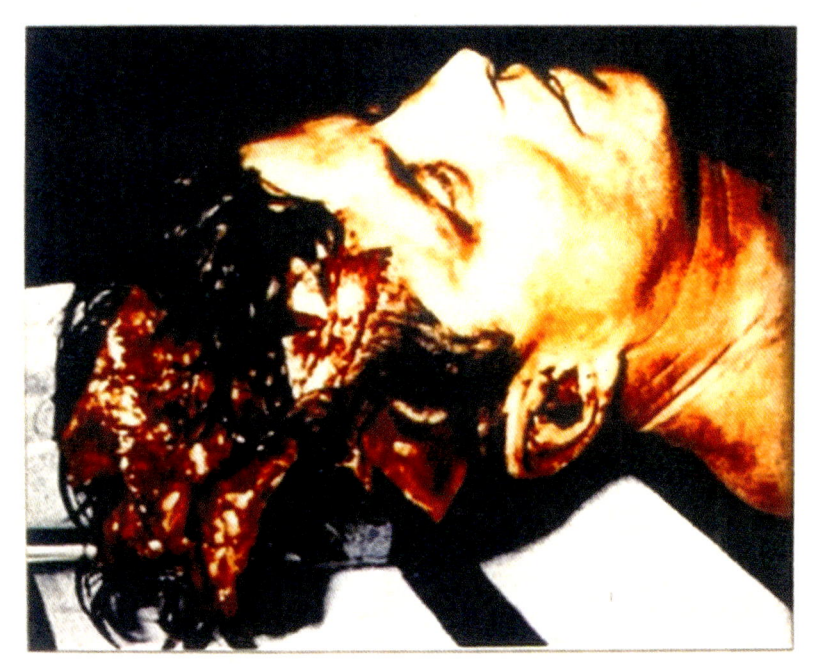

Photo 15-16. Color photo conveys great devastation to the president's head, but his face remains intact. (Source, both photos: US Government Archive)

Acknowledging the nervous system argument (which has not been confirmed but for argument, let's entertain that it could be)—it would be a moot point, eliminated by this next forensic fact:

The WC noted the damage to the skeletal recreations left ALL of them with half a face, the same as they claim happened to JFK but which is easily and inarguably contrasted in his autopsy photos, which are now in public domain, where you—you yourself with your own eyes—can see clearly that his face is injury free.

Believe the Unrefuted Facts

The fourth shot, according to straightforward ballistics, forensics, physics, math—whatever your irrefutable weapon of choice—all confirm it would have to have been fired from in front of JFK in close proximity to the stockade fence while he was sitting upright in the limo, striking him high in his temple above his right ear causing his head to snap back violently to his left and backward. Now that's the match, set, point the CIA was looking for earlier—but not the one it reported. Ever.

CHAPTER 7

Making My Case

I could continue to present this evidence as a bystander, researcher, or Joe Q. Public, which is valid enough as what we've gone over so far is public access and easily confirmable. But I've promised you a deeper dive than you could Google. I promised you the inside story and my personal access and assessment along with the gentlemen I've spent so much time introducing and trusting. So why don't we step into my office?

My assignment commenced in earnest during the early weeks of January 1977. As congressionally conceived, the HSCA, as a Select Committee, had an investigative life of two years, winding up at midnight on December 31, 1978.

However, in this case, I made it quite clear to the HSCA Committee members *regarding the conduct of my probe, the search for truth must not be compromised by politics, bias, inclinations, or the dictates of our passions. The immutable facts, those and only those not capable of refutation, will predominate and be reported to the public.*

The HSCA members assured me that they would support such an investigation and not interfere politically or otherwise. Unfortunately, after just three months, the Committee reneged and broke its word, violating its hands-off commitment. In so doing, it demeaned and fractured our attempts to conduct a trustworthy search for truth. This HSCA-despoiling misconduct would result in Sprague's and my resignations in an instant. If the truth was to be buried and misdirection to be reported, neither I nor Sprague would be caught dead standing at a mic delivering the deception, nor hiding in the dark, holding the shovel.

As an ADA in the DAO, I had been accustomed to debunking beyond doubt so-called conspiracy theories proffered by defense attorneys during major, high-profile murder cases that I prosecuted. Many of those types of cases and trials are the subject matters I tell in the stories in my twenty-nine published novels, featuring the Butch Karp/Marlene Ciampi thrillers and four nonfiction dramas.

The House Select Committee on Assassinations (HSCA) was tasked with the responsibility for the congressional investigations into the deaths of JFK and MLK.

Richard A. Sprague was designated as chief counsel and staff director and appointed me as deputy chief counsel in charge of the subcommittee inquiry into the assassination of JFK. Another subcommittee was responsible for the Reverend Dr. Martin Luther King assassination report. But for the president, I would be working with someone I trusted with my life and who I believed would say the same of me. At least, he trusted me with the Truth, and that's what we were both committed to, no matter what that

Making My Case 77

meant. No matter what we found or who we'd have to face, we would let the evidence speak for itself.

First, let's take a glimpse at some of that convincing and convicting, immutable evidence.

The Truth—Dealey Plaza

We learned from the evidence that five shots were fired in Dealey Plaza, not three as asserted by the WC. The five shots took just 8.3 seconds and were disbursed in two flurries: the first three shots were fired in 2.6 seconds and struck JFK and Governor Connally in the back. Immediately thereafter, the shooting ceased for 4.8 seconds. Then at Zapruder film frame 313 (Z313), the fourth shot, causing a boom blast from the front right knoll hill stockade fence area in close proximity to where Zapruder was filming, struck JFK in his temple above his right ear. This shot caused JFK's head to violently snap back and to the left leaving him immobile, bodily depressed, and slumped dead, leaning into Mrs. Kennedy's right shoulder. Within seven-tenths of a second, immediately thereafter, the fifth shot fired from behind JFK struck him in the cowlick (high top) of his head that enlarged the deadly avulsive head wound, creating a larger flap at the side of his head that cratered over his right ear area. The fifth shot also caused his head to move forward, starting at Zapruder frames 327–328 through Zapruder frames 337 et seq.

The fourth and fatal shot killed the president.

That shot was fired from in front of JFK, behind the stockade fence in close proximity to the knoll hill just to the right where Abraham Zapruder was filming the event. The fatal shot not only caused JFK to simultaneously at impact snap his head violently back and to his left, but also blew out the lower rear of his head

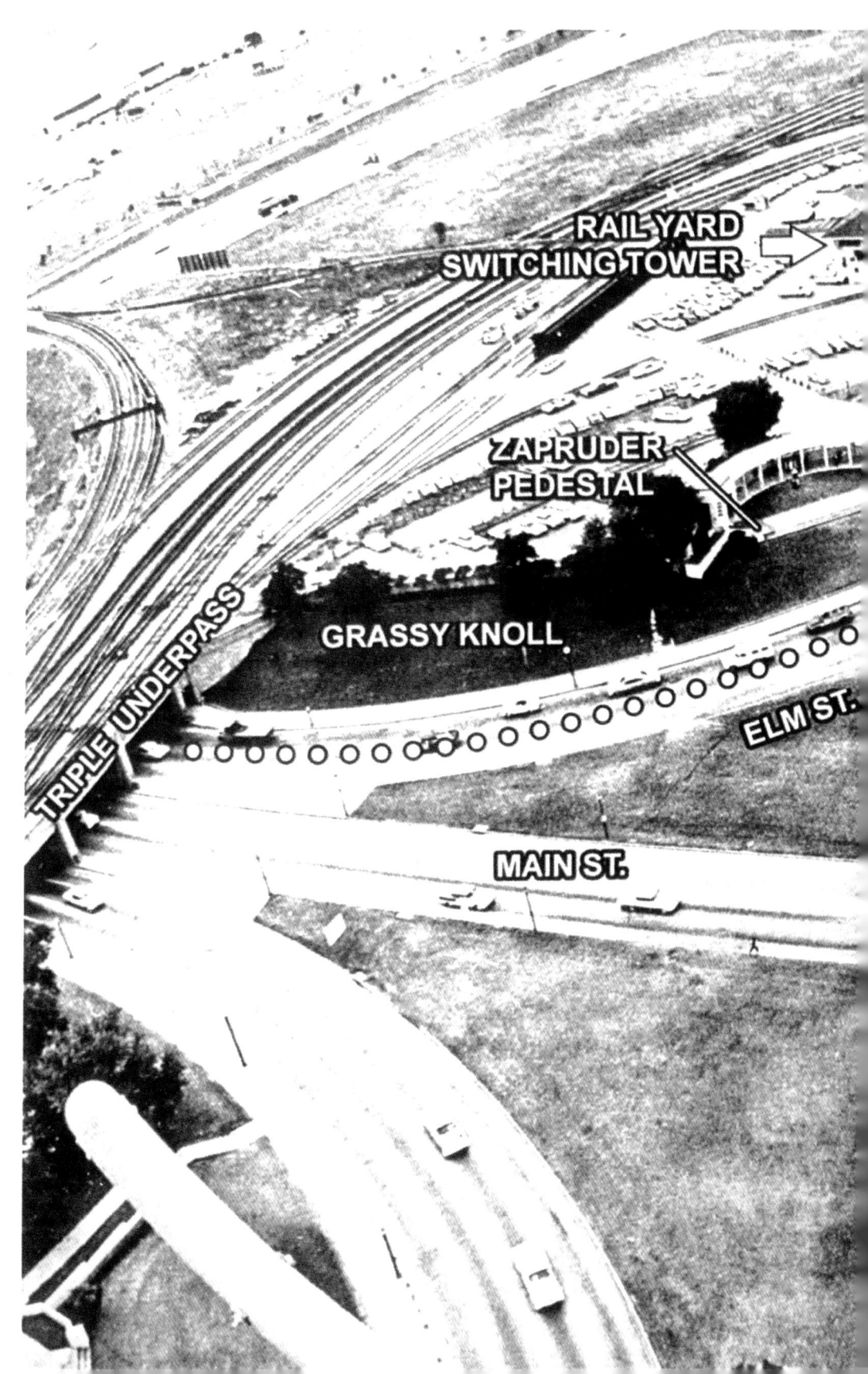

RAIL YARD SWITCHING TOWER →

ZAPRUDER PEDESTAL

TRIPLE UNDERPASS

GRASSY KNOLL

ELM ST.

MAIN ST.

(Photo courtesy of Josiah Thompson)

where the parietal and occipital portions of the skull in the back of the head are joined.

This corroboration of the fourth shot, the fatal blast fired from the knoll hill stockade fence area, includes:

Witnesses and Exhibits
Scene witnesses on both sides of Elm Street including those on the railway overpass bridge and in the railway switching tower:

S. M. Holland, Plus Five Others
Holland was the supervising director of the personnel working the railway switching tower. He was watching the events from the railway overpass bridge with the five others who worked the functioning of the switching tower operation. They all then observed the first flurry of shots that struck both Governor Connally and JFK in the back.

Shortly thereafter, they heard a boom blast—the fourth Shot—and turned to their left, viewing the stockade fence area

Photo 5-5. Holland on overpass during assassination as Mrs. Kennedy crawls to back of vehicle. (AP photo/James W. "Ike" Altgens)

Photo 5-4. Holland on overpass pointing towards fence. Note Bowers's location to the left—at the railway switching tower. (Photo courtesy of Josiah Thompson)

Photo 5-9. Holland standing behind the stockade fence.
(Photo courtesy of Josiah Thompson)

where the boom blast had originated. They then focused their attention back to JFK who they saw seated in the limo mortally wounded, physically immobile, and leaning on Mrs. Kennedy's right shoulder.

Lee Bowers
Bowers was working the railway switching tower, heard the shot, and observed a flash of light and smoke as a result of the rifle shot.

Emmett Hudson and Bill and Gayle Newman
These three witnesses claimed that they were in the line of fire emanating from the knoll hill stockade fence area, which was directly behind them.

Photo 4-4. Newmans on ground after shooting. (Photo by Wilma Bond)

Police Officer Joe Marshall Smith
Officer Smith confronts a man at the stockade fence who self IDs as a Secret Service agent, but all of the Secret Service agents were in the motorcade.

Associated Press Photographer, James Altgens

Altgens was standing on the south side of Elm Street photographing the president, who was sitting upright while the limo was rolling down Elm in a westerly direction towards him. At the time of the boom blast, Altgens was readying his camera for a close-up shot. As he maneuvered, he missed the fourth shot. He saw JFK was no longer sitting upright but was at that point immobile, seated in the limo leaning against Mrs. Kennedy's right shoulder. His detailed description of JFK post the fourth shot accurately described the aftermath of the impact of the shot.

Charles Brehm

Brehm was on the south side of Elm Street standing with his five-year-old son watching the president's limo, which was on Elm Street moving westerly towards him. He recalled that as the limo approached, JFK had just been shot in the back. As the limo passed him, he noticed JFK still sitting upright but bracing with his fists alongside his shoulders. As the limo made its way down Elm Street away from him, he heard another shot ring out which he recalled blew out JFK's head. Naturally, here he describes the fourth shot fired down the street from him. Then suddenly he heard another shot. This one raced past him. He wondered why. The assassin already murdered the president by blowing out his head. Why was it necessary to continue the shooting? He figured from his experience that perhaps there was going to be an uncontrolled shoot-out, so he placed his son on the ground and covered him.

Brehm was an expert on gunshots. He was an American Ranger of Pointe du Hoc where he fought for two weeks at Normandy and was wounded by gunshot. (see Appendix 3) He may have miscounted the number of shots, but he was definite about the shots JFK first took to his back in the first flurry, then the deadly devastating boom blast, the fourth shot which he misconstrues as the second shot, that blew out JFK's head.

Mary Moorman

Moorman documents the "anomalous shape" in her photo taken 1/10 second after the fourth shot from the stockade fence at the knoll hill. NOTE: The "anomalous shape" in the Moorman photo after the fourth shot is consistent with the Holland observation of the boom blast fourth shot from the stockade fence. Someone is clearly in view in the shots fired confines.

Photo 3-9. Moorman photograph with shot trajectory. (Photo by Mary Ann Moorman / Public Domain)

Motorcade Police Officers Flanking the President's Limo

Police Officer Bobby Hargis, riding on the Mrs. Kennedy side of the limo, was debris-splattered with blood, brain, and bone.

Police Officer Douglas Jackson, riding on the JFK side, was not similarly impacted. After Police Officer Bobby Hargis was showered with debris, he jumped from his motorcycle and ran across the street to the North side of Elm to the stockade fence knoll hill site from which the shots were fired.

Photo 4-3. Officer Hargis turns toward knoll. (Photo by Wilma Bond)

Secret Service Agent Clint Hill
Hill, who jumped onto the tail end of the presidential limo, was splattered with debris and observed the avulsive wound as a gaping hole in the back of the president's head.

Scientific Audio and Visual Evidence
Acoustic experts at Bolt Baranack & Newman based in Cambridge, Massachusetts (a partnership of Richard Bolt, Leo Beranek, and Robert Newman), and the Queens College Department of Computer Sciences originated their investigations from Police Officer McClain's motorcycle recording device, Acoustics. Fifteen

Photo 15-5. Frame Z 334—Note creamy red spot on Secret Service agent Clint Hill's right forehead.

Photos 15-6 and 15-7. Frame Z 335 and Z 337. These clearer frames in the sequence show the spot on Hill's forehead.

(Photos this page: Zapruder Film © The Sixth Floor Museum at Dealey Plaza)

years later, that investigation corroborates what witnesses told law enforcement within one hour of the assassination.

Doctors and Trauma Room 1 Personnel

Dr. Kemp Clark, Chief of Neurosurgery, observed a gaping hole in the back of JFK's head. "The lower right occipital bone was blown out and I saw the cerebellum." It was Dr. Clark who pronounced JFK dead at 1:00 p.m., November 22nd.

The Parkland Doctors

This team of doctors was tasked with assessing the head wounds and attempting whatever measures possible to save JFK's life:

Dr. Robert McClelland of Parkland Hospital drafted a vivid diagram depicting the gaping hole in the back of JFK's head.

Dr. Malcolm Perry annotated a "large avulsive injury of the right occipitoparietal area" and was threatened by a government official if he ever stated again that the "wound of entry" was at the throat!

Dr. Marion Jenkins thought the avulsive wound was an exit wound in the rear of JFK's head; the doctors had in fact used a retractor to aid in viewing the avulsive head wound. Note: JFK's head always moved in the consistent direction of the force applied. So, when he is hit by the fourth shot in the temple area above his right ear which came from in front of him from the stockade fence area, his head moves violently to his left and backward landing in Mrs. Kennedy's right shoulder.

Governor Connally's thoracic surgeon, **Dr. Robert Shaw:** notes a "27-degree declination regarding the bullet wound to Connally's back—in and out wound." Note: Dr. Shaw couldn't have known at time of reporting, there is also a 27-degree declination from the rooftop of the County Records building located in the northeastern corner of Elm Street directly to the rear of president's limo to point of entry into Connally's back.

Governor Connally's wrist surgeon, **Dr. Charles Gregory:** A field surgeon with First Marines in Korea, Gregory worked on over 500 gunshot wound cases and noted that Governor Connally was struck with a sharp-edged fragment. Some small fragments in Connally's wrist were removed for comparison with the so-called magic bullet Commission Exhibit 399 (CE 399). Connally's wound shattered his wrist's radial nerve and cut fully the tendon leading from his right thumb to his index finger. It must be noted that during all the shots fired up to this point, Connally was holding onto his white Stetson hat. As a result of these wounds, Dr.

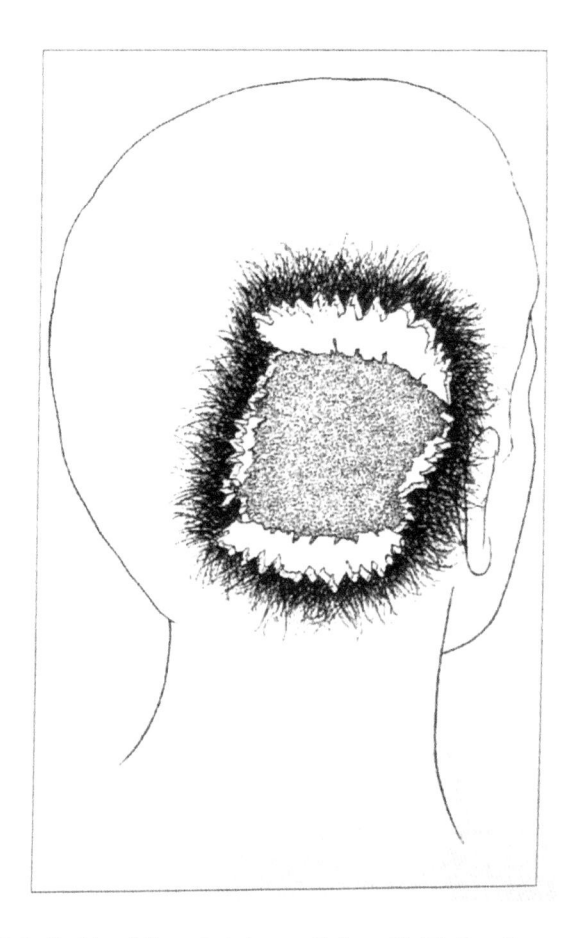

Figure 15-3. Parkland Hospital doctor Robert McClelland's wound description as drawn by a medical illustrator. Dr. McClelland later declared the sketch to be accurate. (Photo courtesy of Josiah Thompson)

Gregory found that Governor Connally would no longer be able to hold onto the white Stetson hat which, in fact, he had released at Z frame 328.

* * *

If the government's case rests upon evidence, it falls far short of the extent of evidence which would be necessary to obtain a conviction of LHO in any court in America—legally speaking, cut and dry. Once the prosecution surrenders the moral high ground, it substantially diminishes its likelihood of success.

Through my Committee service and role in leading the congressional investigation, I have been afforded exceptional access and uniquely equipped to provide these stunning and shocking "immutable facts" that reveal unequivocally that the government's reliance on the Warren Commission (WC) investigation and the HSCA alleged probe were reprehensively and ultimately gut-wrenchingly misleading and downright dishonest.

In a "mock trial" conducted at the South Texas College of Law, Houston on Thursday, November 16, 2017, by invitation, I represented the case against the government in the presidential assassination. At that mock trial, it was confoundingly disappointing to see the degree to which the government's case was a putatively pathetic regurgitation of the false narrative it has propounded for the past sixty years. That's not a relative opinion but a culmination of absolutes—an actual impossibility to draw any other conclusion unless you are intending to deceive.

I was assisted in that process by the inimitable Josiah Thompson, who provided me publicly with exhibits I've contained herein and which I used during my Houston presentation. Thompson believed in the importance of Kennedy assassination researchers' freedom and ability to share information obtained with colleagues similarly situated. He's authored *Last Second in Dallas*, which I recommend to you.

We've already seen that the government's evidence has been indelibly rendered scientifically invalid and otherwise inherently unworthy of belief (and we've not even seen it all quite yet), but further, as you will momentarily discover, this was neither naïve nor a complication of misinterpretation. It was an intricately intentional contrivance. This was a shoddy attempt at sleight of hand, and you don't even have to look closely. It's humiliatingly obvious.

CHAPTER 8

Decentralized Intelligence Government Duplicities and Complex Contrivances

In December 1963, shortly after the assassination, the Secret Service and FBI found that Connally and JFK were struck by two separate bullets. They also determined that they were both shot within 1.9 seconds of each other.

Here's the Problem

The manual bolt action necessary to fire separate successive shots from the alleged murder weapon, the Mannlicher Carcano rifle, takes 2.3 seconds: ergo—the Mannlicher Carcano could not have fired both shots. Now confronted with the absence of its

Mannlicher Carcano rifle, the CIA in March of 1964 ordered that a one bullet theory would still support its predetermined outcome—three shots fired from the sixth floor alleged "sniper's nest" window inside the Book Depository building by the lone gunman, LHO. However, the evidence continuously shows that the one bullet theory is a sham, a fabrication, and scientifically invalid.

Further Corroboration of the Fourth Shot

Bethesda witnesses at autopsy including three autopsists, two FBI agents, three Secret Service agents, five technicians, a Navy corpsman and mortician, et al., all observed a gaping hole in the rear of JFK's head and through memorializations, so informed the HSCA, totally contrary to HSCA Forensic Medical Panel report.

Minute Metallic Fragments

The three skull x-rays from these examinations show minute metallic fragments inside JFK's right side of his skull ranging from high in the right temple area through the rear region.

Also, the X-rays show a spatially consistent, fuzzy gray cloud near the center of the fragment trail that extends across the top of the skull. This "cloud" and its placement in the tract tell us the *direction and point of entry* of the fatal boom blast of the last, fourth shot. Moreover, the "Minute Metallic" fragments make up a kind of missile dust and stay where they were formed; in this case, near the impact point above JFK's right temple.

The Pretense Probe

It is of vital national historical importance that these factually accurate pieces of evidence be revealed in this context. In so doing, we come to understand that the government knowingly contrived a *predetermined conclusion* through the *pretense of an investigation*.

Decentralized Intelligence . . . 93

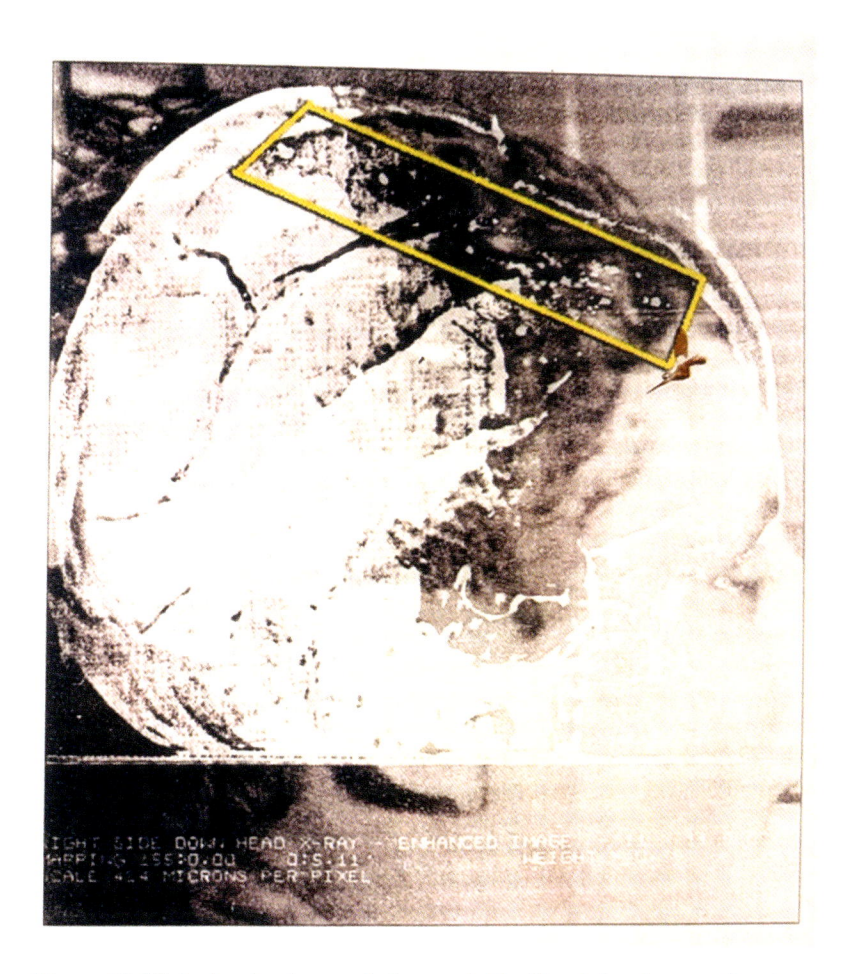

Figure 15-18. Lateral autopsy photo overlaid with a lateral x-ray showing trail of multiple minute metallic fragments, which indicates the direction and point of entry of the wound from the front side of JFK's head. (Source: US Government Archive)

This predetermined outcome required both the WC and HSCA to disregard all the convincing and trustworthy evidence to the contrary.

The absolutists who still support the WC, it's fair to say, are immune from reason, facts, and evidence that totally refutes the

WC and HSCA predetermined outcomes. Just as I present iron-clad trustworthy corroboration for the fourth fatal shot fired from in front of JFK in the knoll hill stockade fence area, there is also significant convincing and corroborating evidence that the fifth shot, fired seven tenths of a second after the fourth shot, came from the northeast building complex area located at Houston and Elm Streets.

It's a proven and accepted fact that LHO was nowhere near the stockade fence at the time the fatal shots were fired. The WC has LHO, at all times relevant, in the sixth-floor sniper's nest inside the Book Depository.

To determine the significance of the existence of the fifth shot and the fragments that came forward as a result, I was assisted in this inquiry by Robert J. Groden, photographic consultant for the HSCA. He is truly a remarkable individual with enormous knowledge of diagnosing the photographic evidence of the video material he gathered, aided by staff members.

We knew that at Zapruder frame 255 (Z255), which appears after the first flurry of three shots, shows no limo damage to the interior windshield to the left of the rearview mirror. Remember JFK and Governor Connally had both been hit already by the time you reach Zapruder frames 224-230.

As we looked at the Zapruder film, we did not detect a flare that would have been seen if the limo had been damaged. Yet, we did see at the end of viewing the Zapruder film the damage to the left of the rear-view mirror. It was not sufficient for us to simply say "the damage was there, so be it," so I asked Groden how we can show it happened without seeing the flare, similar to the type of flare at Z313 showing the enormous impact to the right side of JFK's head.

Groden agreed that we must go frame by frame. Indeed, we did, and at Zapruder frame 328 (Z328), there was a flare resulting from the impact of a fragment that damaged the interior of the limo windshield to the left of the rearview.

Once we knew unequivocally of the bullet fragment at Z328, it became apparent that the fifth shot struck JFK's cowlick at the top of his head with fragments therefrom causing the following effects:

1. The impact of the shot caused JFK's head to move forward.
2. The resulting impact wound from the shot enlarged the existing head wound caused by the fourth shot.
3. The fragment clearly damaged the limo interior windshield to the left of the rearview.
4. Another fragment struck Connally in the right wrist that severed the tendon between his right thumb and index finger, causing Connally to drop his Stetson.

HSCA's Fractured Truth

One of the most egregious overt acts of indefensible government duplicity occurred in the late summer of 1978. The HSCA was set to expire on December 31, 1978. As a House Select Committee, it had a two-year life and started to circulate its Executive Findings in its various fields of inquiry.

At page 37 of the HSCA's Forensic Medical Panel Report, HSCA, in substance, concluded that, "regarding the gaping hole in the back of the president's head, the Parkland doctors must have been mistaken because all of the twenty-six witnesses present at the autopsy of JFK in Bethesda observed no gaping hole in the back of the president's head."

HSCA, at its expiration, sealed its investigative records for fifty years.

Revelation of Truth: The Records Act

In 1992, Congress passed the **JFK Records Act**, and in 1993 the Assassination Records Review Board administered the release of various records.

As we introduced in the last chapter, at least twenty of the Bethesda witnesses had informed HSCA in memorializations that they in fact had observed the gaping hole in the back of JFK's head. They and the Parkland doctors, along with dozens of other witnesses, observed the gaping hole in the back of JFK's head.

So why would the HSCA Report level this false accusation at the Parkland doctors? Because the HSCA top brass who crafted the forensic medical panel's factually manipulated **Summary Report** understood that if you believe the Parkland doctors, who not only observed the gaping hole but also noted that it was an exit wound resulting from the shot from the front knoll hill stockade fence area, then you would have to conclude that the government's sixty-year-old narrative is a total (and brazen) fabrication—that LHO could not and did not shoot and kill JFK.

It's one thing to make that claim, it's another to prove it. We've done that in spades already, but there is still more that provides the proverbial nail in the coffin when we look at the finer points of reporting, chain of custody, etcetera.

Chain of Possession/Custody of CE399—the Magic Bullet of the One Bullet Theory

- Darrell Tomlinson—found the bullet on the stretcher unconnected to care of Governor Connally or JFK and gives it to →
- O.P. Wright—Parkland Hospital security director and former deputy chief of police in Dallas [NOTE: O. P. Wright always maintained that the bullet he received from Darrell

Decentralized Intelligence . . .   97

Photo 14-03. Frame Z 328 with bullet trajectory (red), fragment trajectory to Connally (white) and windshield fragment trajectory (yellow). (Zapruder Film © The Sixth Floor Museum at Dealey Plaza)

Photo 14-81. Frame Z 329. (Zapruder Film © The Sixth Floor Museum at Dealey Plaza)

Decentralized Intelligence . . . 99

Photo 14-82.
Frame Z330.
(Zapruder Film ©
The Sixth Floor
Museum at Dealey
Plaza)

Tomlinson was with a "pointed tip," not cylindrical, not rounded.]—who in turn gives it to →
- Secret Service Agent Richard Johnsen →
- Secret Service Chief, James Rawley in DC →
- FBI Elmer Todd →
- FBI Robert Frazier—expert analyst

In 1967, the government released a 34-page letterhead memo dated 7/7/64. It purported to show that on 6/12/64, FBI agent Bardwell Odum went to Parkland Hospital and showed CE399, the pristine bullet, to Tomlinson and Wright. They allegedly told Odum that the bullet looked similar to the one Tomlinson found on the stretcher in Parkland Hospital. When Odum was interviewed, he stated that he never had possession of CE399, never spoke to Tomlinson or Wright, and never went to Parkland Hospital!

CIA Culture and Its Role in Duplicity

The President Harry S. Truman memo of Sunday, December 22, 1963, published in the *Washington Post,* attested that Truman believed and documented that it was a big mistake to have permitted the Office of Strategic Services (OSS) to morph into the creation of the CIA. Truman's objections were that the CIA engaged in the following misconduct.

1. Created independent policy.
2. Executed that policy both diplomatically and militarily, with or without accountability.

Below is the full transcription of the memo, which is also added as Appendix 1 in its original form.

Limit CIA Role To Intelligence
by Harry S. Truman
December 22, 1963
The Washington Post
[approved for release 2004/12/15]

INDEPENDENCE, MO., Dec. 21[2]—I think it has become necessary to take another look at the purpose and operations of our Central Intelligence Agency—CIA. At least, I would like to submit here the original reason why I thought it necessary to organize this Agency during my Administration, what I expected it to do and how it was to operate as an arm of the President.

I think it is fairly obvious that by and large a President's performance in office is as effective as the information he has and the information he gets. That is to say, that assuming the President himself possesses a knowledge of our history, a sensitive understanding of our institutions, and an insight into the needs and aspirations of the people, he needs to have available to him the most accurate and up-to-the-minute information on what is going on everywhere in the world, and particularly of the trends and developments in all the danger spots in the contest between East and West. This is an immense task and requires a special kind of an intelligence facility.

Of course, every President has available to him all the information gathered by the many intelligence agencies already in existence. The Departments of State, Defense, Commerce, Interior and others are constantly engaged in extensive information gathering and have done excellent work.

---

2   Truman's original version was syndicated by the North American Newspaper Alliance on December 21 and 22, 1963. This truncated version was run as an op-ed in the *Washington Post* on December 22.

But their collective information reached the President all too frequently in conflicting conclusions. At times, the intelligence reports tended to be slanted to conform to established positions of a given department. This becomes confusing and what's worse, such intelligence is of little use to a President in reaching the right decisions.

Therefore, I decided to set up a special organization charged with the collection of all intelligence reports from every available source, and to have those reports reach me as President without department "treatment" or interpretations.

I wanted and needed the information in its "natural raw" state and in as comprehensive a volume as it was practical for me to make full use of it. But the most important thing about this move was to guard against the chance of intelligence being used to influence or to lead the President into unwise decisions—and I thought it was necessary that the President do his own thinking and evaluating.

Since the responsibility for decision making was his—then he had to be sure that no information is kept from him for whatever reason at the discretion of any one department or agency, or that unpleasant facts be kept from him. There are always those who would want to shield a President from bad news or misjudgments to spare him from being "upset."

For some time I have been disturbed by the way CIA has been diverted from its original assignment. It has become an operational and at times a policy-making arm of the Government. This has led to trouble and may have compounded our difficulties in several explosive areas.

I never had any thought that when I set up the CIA that it would be injected into peacetime cloak and dagger operations. Some of the complications and embarrassment I think we have experienced are in part attributable to the fact that this quiet intelligence arm of the

Decentralized Intelligence . . .

President has been so removed from its intended role that it is being interpreted as a symbol of sinister and mysterious foreign intrigue—and a subject for cold war enemy propaganda.

With all the nonsense put out by Communist propaganda about "Yankee imperialism," "exploitive capitalism," "war-mongering," "monopolists," in their name-calling assault on the West, the last thing we needed was for the CIA to be seized upon as something akin to a subverting influence in the affairs of other people. [emphasis mine]

I well knew the first temporary director of the CIA, Adm. Souers, and the later permanent directors of the CIA, Gen. Hoyt Vandenberg and Allen Dulles. These were men of the highest character, patriotism and integrity—and I assume this is true of all those who continue in charge.

But there are now some searching questions that need to be answered. I, therefore, would like to see the CIA be restored to its original assignment as the intelligence arm of the President, and that whatever else it can properly perform in that special field—and that its operational duties be terminated or properly used elsewhere.

We have grown up as a nation, respected for our free institutions and for our ability to maintain a free and open society. There is something about the way the CIA has been functioning that is casting a shadow over our historic position and I feel that we need to correct it.

In fact, the CIA was charged with the responsibility of fact-finding re: National Defense and providing the investigative facts to the White House responsible for setting policy and ensuring its legal implementation.

The John McCone letter, dated March 3, 1964, re: Central Intel Report on the Assassination of JFK from Mr. John McCone,

CIA Director to Mr. James Rowley, Chief of the Secret Service, talks about, inter alia, McCone's concern about the following:

Vital information re: office leaks; sensitive information had by Mr. Hoover of the FBI; conduct regarding Lee Harvey Oswald's activities and subversive training; and most importantly his concern that vital sensitive information be protected. For example, he stated in paragraph 6,

> I am concerned that if this information were in any way disclosed to the wrong persons it would lead the media to erroneously claim this agency and perhaps others were directly involved in the Dallas action. While the persons involved were in the employ of this agency as well as the Federal Bureau of Investigation, it is virtually impossible for this or any agency to maintain full 24 hour a day responsibility over its operatives.

Below is the full transcription of the McCone letter, which is also added as Appendix 2 in its original form.

Memorandum
DATE March 3, 1964
C0-2-34, 030
Mr. James J. Rowley
Chief, U.S. Secret Service

Mr. John McCone
Director, Central Intelligence Agency

ECT: Central Intelligence Report on the Assassination of John Kennedy

Decentralized Intelligence . . .

In response to the request made by your office on 24 February 1964 re: Lee Oswald's activities and assignments on behalf of this agency and Federal Bureau of Investigation, there follows a narrative summary of the internal subversive activities of the Oswald subject.

I recommend that unless the Commission makes a specific request for specific information contained herein, that this information not be volunteered. This agency has reason to assume that some junior Commission staff members may be potential sources of leaks to the news media or to other agencies; due to the highly sensitive nature of the enclosed material, it would certainly be in the national interest to withhold it at this time – unless there is, of course, a specific request made.

It is my understanding that Mr. Hoover has certain sensitive information within his agency, which has been transferred to his own personal files for safekeeping; he concurs that no material should be voluntarily given to the Commission which might affect the status of field operatives or their safety. He is particularly concerned about the De Bruey memorandum, which Central Intelligence has obtained and which, I understand, you have obtained. It is imperative that this information, at least for the time, remain under wraps.

Oswald subject was trained by this agency, under cover of the Office of Naval Intelligence, for Soviet assignments. During preliminary training, in 1957, subject was active in aerial reconnaissance of mainland China and maintained a security clearance up to the clearance up to the "confidential" level. His military records during this period are open to your agency and I have directed they be forwarded to the Commission.

Subject received additional indoctrination at our own Camp Peary site from September 8 to October 17, 1958, and participated in a few relatively minor assignments until arrangements were made for his entry to the Soviet Union in September 1959. While in the Soviet Union, he was on special assignment in the area of Minsk, it would not be advantageous at this time to divulge the specifics of that assignment; however, if you wish this information, it can be made available for your personal inspection within the confines of our own offices, or I can send it by courier on the condition that it not leave the custody of the courier. *I am concerned that if this information were in any way disclosed to the wrong persons it would lead the media to erroneously claim this agency and perhaps others, were directly involved in the Dallas action. While the persons involved were in the employ of this agency as well as the Federal Bureau of Investigation, it is virtually impossible for this or any agency to maintain full 24-hour-a-day responsibility over its operatives.*[emphasis mine]

At the time of the Dallas action, the Oswald subject was only seldom in our employ; after the Soviet assignment, we found him to be unreliable and emotionally unstable. He was of little use to us after his marriage and De Bruey, from what I understand, concurs in this. He was provided with a few unimportant infiltration assignments and proved of little or no value.

It is possible that Oswald, given his instability, might have been involved in some operation concerning Hoffa, as noted in SAIC Bertram's report to your agency dated 1/3/64. Mr. Hoover advises that his agency is trying to determine whether Hoffa might have been involved laterally or vertically with the Dallas assassination. I have advised that I would be interested in seeing the results of that investigation.

Mr. Hoover advises that the facts given in SAIC Bertram's 1/3/64 report are basically correct; his agency has advised Deputy Sweatt against further unauthorized statements to the news media which might adversely effect the investigation. Mr. Hoover advises he has no knowledge of how Deputy Sweatt obtained his information, as there is no record of the agency distributing any such information to Sweatt or any other member of Dallas Sherriff's office. It is regrettable that this information has come to the attention of the news media, but I am sure Mr. Hoover will be able to clarify the situation.

Speculation within this agency – and this is only speculation at this point – is that the Oswald subject became unstable following surgery April 1, 1961, in the Minsk Hospital. He may have been chemically or electronically "controlled" . . . a sleeper agent. Subject spent eleven days hospitalized for a "minor ailment" which should have required no more than three days hospitalization at the most. Six days after his release, he met Marina Prusakova. This agency is particularly interested in her intelligence background, and I have requested a report on same from our Soviet Embassy contact.

After his return to the U.S., Oswald worked in New Orleans through The Anti-Communist League of the Caribbean and Friends of Democratic Cuba, his case officer was SAIC Guy Bannister, from the Chicago FBI office. He was transferred from his assignments there after he was arrested and fined for an incident stemming from his distribution of pamphlets for the Fair Play for Cuba Committee. While our files here show no further assignments or contact, I am requesting an A5 check on the subject from our New Orleans and Ft. Worth offices.

Confidential

Please direct any further communications on this matter to my personal attention so that your requests may be expedited, or feel free to call me anytime. My office is always available to you.

John McCone

In Chairman Stokes's office that day, as I was presenting the findings of the congressional investigation into the presidential assassination, I also continued to present Stokes with the following examples of CIA duplicity:

1. On October 1, 1963, the CIA created a fake LHO who called the Cuban Embassy from inside the Russian Embassy in Mexico City, requesting travel to Havana and then to the Kremlin to his Russian counterparts. The caller identified himself as Lee Henry Oswald. His self-description and photo were on the CIA telex sent out to all CIA executive intel operatives worldwide. The fake Oswald demanded travel visas to both Cuba and Russia.

After finding out that the Telex contained misinformation re: LHO, the CIA never sent out a corrected version. More important, on October 1, 1963, is the question of why the CIA was interested in LHO some seven weeks before the assassination. This fabrication served as a CIA-arranged manipulation to present LHO as an unfriendly "bold actor" (or "bad actor") seeking connection with communist counterparts. In furtherance of that notion, the fake LHO still representing himself as the authentic LHO in a telephone call to the Soviet Consulate, spoke with the Russian Kostikov, notably involved in "wet operations" including assassinations.

On or about a year after the shutdown of the HSCA on December 31, 1978, at the University of Southern California, there was a debate between distinguished counsel, Mark Lane, and the CIA's David Phillips. At the conclusion of the debate, audience members were encouraged to participate in a question-and-answer session.

Abby Mann, the famed producer of theatrical films such as *Judgment at Nuremberg*, asked David Phillips the following question: "Why, Mr. Phillips, do you find it necessary to try and destroy the character of Mark Lane?" In his response, Phillips apologized for his misconduct and submitted a startling admission, and stated unequivocally that the entire Mexico City operation was false—a sham created by the CIA for its own purposes. A means to a very mean end.

> 2. National Archive investigators found incidents where executive intel agents literally *rewrote the testimony of key witnesses* to conform their observations to the single bullet shooter dogma.

Remember that expert metallurgical PhDs revealed that Neutron Activation Analysis (NAA) as previously discussed, consisted in false assumptions concerning bullet composition homogeneity to support its hypothesis because the concept that each bullet has a unique chemical signature is, and was fake, invalid, and discredited. [Interesting to note that NAA tests on paraffin casts of LHO's right cheek corroborated spectrographic tests indicating that LHO had not fired a rifle on November 22, 1963.]

> 3. James Angleton, counter intel czar, ran LHO as a fake defector to the Soviet Union in 1959. LHO had been a CIA asset since 1957. At the time of his recruitment into Angleton's operation, Oswald was a radar operator working at CIA's top-secret Lockheed U2 airbase in Atsugi, Japan. Oswald, a US Marine, had been stationed at Atsugi since 1957, tracking the CIA's spy plane flights over the Soviet Union and China. Oswald was being run by a small, highly compartmentalized CIA counter intel unit responsible only to Angleton who wanted Oswald to flesh out the "mole" at Langley. The "mole" had given the Soviets technical radar information

enabling the Soviets to shoot down Francis Gary Powers's U2 spy plane.

As part of the plan to find the "mole," Oswald entered the American Embassy in Moscow and loudly announced he was renouncing his American citizenship and turning over classified radar information to the Russians. The hope was that the Langley "mole" would contact Oswald. He didn't!

4. When Oswald was returning to the US in 1962, the State Department issued him and his wife, Marina, visas and funded their return. He was never debriefed, no FBI investigation or Department of Justice inquiry.

Moreover, George de Mohrenschildt, a white Russian aristocrat, wealthy businessman, and fervent anti-communist, befriended Oswald. He became Oswald's caretaker and squired him for about the next six months while Oswald was in Dallas. De Mohrenschildt had a close relationship with Harold Byrd, a rightwing Dallas oilman and co-founder of the Civil Air Patrol where Oswald trained as a cadet. Byrd despised JFK and owned the Texas School Book Depository where, six weeks before the assassination, CIA operative, Ruth Paine, obtained Oswald's employment. Byrd was also close to Air Force General Charles Cabell, a CIA deputy director, and Bay of Pigs organizer. JFK fired Cabell after the Bay of Pigs debacle. Cabell's brother was Dallas Mayor Earle Cabell, who helped pick and disseminate the motorcade route through Dealey Plaza.

He was also deemed a CIA asset.

I had particular interest in George de Mohrenschildt. He clearly had vital information about LHO, according to my sources/informants. To ensure his cooperation, I approved Gaetan Fonzi to serve a subpoena on him that required him to be questioned by me in the Grand Jury.

Fonzi was a highly respected, competent investigative journalist who had worked for Dick Sprague in Philadelphia. Fonzi served the subpoena as directed. Shortly thereafter, de Mohrenschildt, at his southern east coast Florida home, placed a loaded gun in his mouth and sadly ended his life—the local DA informed me that officially his cause of death was by gunshot, and ruled a suicide.

CHAPTER 9

Evidentiary Culmination

Perhaps the most powerful piece of evidence in the whole story came in the form of a straightforward admission from John McCone, the Director of Central Intelligence who replaced Dulles on November 29, 1961. McCone would later write a letter in 1964 in which he admits that people in the CIA murdered the president—the president, by the way, who appointed him to the position. There was loyalty there and he wasn't going to stay quiet. That's what put him in this fraternity of honesty and voices pushing the truth up a hill—whether Capitol Hill or that "City on a Hill"—trying to make right what we've gotten wrong here.

One last person who understood this mantle and chased its worth with us was Cyril Wecht, a medical examiner in Pittsburgh. He was an incredible person. Cyril ate and breathed this case.

It's bizarre how close we became—all these people who knew and stood their ground and took a position against corruption and falsification. Bizarre because these were not traditionally friendly people looking to make friends. Yet, for forty years enduring all this stuff—the kind of thing most don't see, do, or go through—we lived and breathed things that will tie you together. We shared information we had, so we were a needed source when information was usually hidden or killed. Wecht, Sprague, Hogan. It was truly a blessing to know these men and carry these torches through the alleyways of justice.

Wecht Letter

I got a chance to connect with each of these "main characters" in different ways in later years about the investigation—or the life we were each called to lead. Hogan, I visited regularly; Sprague, I sent an evidentiary letter of support reasserting the Truth of certain matters; and to Wecht, I wrote the following for his wife Sigrid at the time of his passing:

> He rendered brilliant analyses regarding extremely sensitive cases of immense importance, most particularity the investigation into the assassination of President Kennedy.
>
> Cyril has been credited deservedly for presenting unimpeachable immutable evidence that beyond any and all doubt explains that the government has been shockingly disingenuous to the American public regarding the case. Simply, our government has been acting sordidly in its blatant alleged pathetic conclusions. Its cover ups just don't work. Cyril's expert analysis rebuts the government's officious deceit. For Cyril, to him, it's all about the truth, as it has always been.
>
> On January 1, 1977, I was appointed deputy chief counsel in charge of the federal investigation into the

assassination of President Kennedy. As a result of my tenure, the two best things that I accomplished at the time were to hire Cyril Wecht and thereafter because of government chicanery, quit!

As you can imagine, I can go on and on relating the true greatness of all that he has done reflecting his search for truth and enormous profound professionalism. During his last year, he would call me virtually every Sunday prior to the traditional family dinner. How special!

Assuredly, those who truly knew him understand that he was, and will always be, the model "Man for all seasons." Notwithstanding all the titles bestowed upon him, the enormity of the pressures created from his significant career and all the accolades he has received, he most appreciated being called Dad and Grandpa at the Sunday night family affairs.

To be sure, today I still mourn. Yet, I know that l will forever miss him.

Mr. Chief Medical Examiner, rest easy, you are with the Lord!

Sprague Letter:

I had reason to write to Dick Sprague when I read some of the facts not matching our first-person experience and the eye-witness accounts that are our careers and lives. That letter became a bit of a summation of all of this—the big picture, in the details. In part, it read:

Thank you for sending me the Jim Beasley book entitled *Courtroom Cowboy.* I enjoyed it. Beasley was quite the character—accomplished, savvy with street-smarts, coupled with an intense work ethic, reflective of a courtroom winner.

Important to note that the author, Ralph Cipriano, inaccurately reported on page 173 that you were "forced" to resign from the House Select Committee on Assassinations (HSCA) investigating the murders of JFK and MLK. You were never "forced" to resign. Quite the contrary.

The HSCA appointed you chief counsel and staff director. You appointed me deputy chief counsel in charge of the investigation into the assassination of JFK.

The Facts:

During the course of the investigation, significant mainstream media, e.g., the *NYT* and *Washington Post*, published inaccurate and defamatory trash about the HSCA's activities and you, personally. Such reportage was shameful in the extreme. It was simply an attempt to disparage and render dissolute the legitimacy of our investigation.

I will always attest to your absolute integrity, excellence and pursuit of truth based upon intensive diligence in search of trustworthy and persuasive evidence. Having been trained and mentored by legendary District Attorney Frank S. Hogan, and his two finest assistants, former Supreme Court Justice Mel Glass, and now deceased Federal District Court Judge in the Southern District of New York, John F. Keenan [now deceased], I know about what it takes to search for truth and can unequivocally state that having worked with you, that you are the "fourth musketeer" that I have been blessed to know.

We both left the HSCA because it became oppressively apparent that the HSCA was not and would not pursue the truth. At the tail-end of March 1977, I explained to you that I was going to resign from the HSCA because of the many Committee-engineered roadblocks, frustrations and disappointments we endured during the investigation.

Basically, the HSCA handcuffed and censored our ability to conduct a fair, thorough and comprehensive probe. For example:

1. We needed to recall to the Committee in executive session and place under oath, again, CIA operative and its third ranking member in 1963 in charge of western hemisphere operations, David Phillips who had already committed perjury and contempt before the Committee—the Committee refused to permit us to recall Phillips which seriously undermined our search for truth.
2. The FBI and the CIA stonewalled the Committee. Both agencies refused to cooperate and grant us the opportunity to access their files and unredacted memos regarding the assassination. The CIA, you may recall, postured that not only would it not provide the documents but that we could read redacted materials only at Langley while prohibiting us from photocopying or taking any notes, respectively. We made it resoundingly clear that if these Executive Intelligence Agencies continued to stonewall, then I would have the Committee issue subpoenas and, if necessary, have a Court order compliance. The Committee not only refused but some Committee members praised the agencies for cooperating with our investigation!
3. During the period while I was tracking down the true identity of Maurice Bishop which we determined from the evidence was a nom de guerre used by Phillips, the

Committee stopped paying us and our staff, pulled the plug on our long-distance telephone calls and ended our franking privileges.

The facts, as John Adams said in 1770 during his defense of the British soldiers during the so-called Boston massacre trial, are stubborn things. We met in your office at the end of March '77 and I explained all of the above and more as the reasons why I was resigning. I said then and I repeat now that I would never be part of an insincere investigation. Under these circumstances, we agreed that the search for truth was seriously being compromised.

I had arranged for a meeting in the evening with Chairman Lou Stokes in his office. Some Committee members were present—those I definitely recall were Richardson Pryor, Stu McKinney, and Chris Dodd, perhaps others as well. When we informed them that we were resigning, they all asked you to stay at the helm and continue to lead the investigation. No one told you to resign! When you said that you would stand firm and chose to resign, Lou Stokes asked me to take over as Chief Counsel. You then gave me your blessing. I thanked the members and you for your gracious gesture but had to refuse because it was overwhelmingly clear that the Committee would not seek the truth. You left and I remained to ensure a smooth transition.

Sadly, the Committee maintained that all of the Parkland Hospital doctors attending JFK in trauma room 1 must have been mistaken when they noted that JFK had a gaping hole in the back of his head, specifically in the parietal/occipital area, because all 26 witnesses at the autopsy of JFK at Bethesda allegedly saw no such injury.

Then the HSCA maneuvered to seal the underlying documents, the records, for 50 years.

The records unequivocally reflect that the following witnesses at Bethesda had given memorializations, depositions, and appearances before the Committee indicating that they, like the Parkland Hospital doctors, had seen the gaping hole in the back of the president's head, to wit:

1. The three autopsists
2. Two FBI agents
3. Three Secret Service agents
4. Five technicians
5. One Navy Corpsman
6. One Mortician

To be complete, there exists a witness list in excess of 60 individuals comprised of scene witnesses, Parkland Hospital and Bethesda personnel and observers, all of whom saw the gaping hole in the back of JFK's head.

Thankfully, we both, of our own volition, resigned. While I believed that the Committee would not seek the truth, I didn't forecast unforgiveable blatant fabrications.

May you continue to be blessed in the New Year—with admiration and utmost respect always.

It was my testimony to Sprague, on his behalf, that would become my summary of findings, and my evidentiary culmination that, looking back at it now, gives me peace, that we did what we could do, we did not bury the truth, we were responsible for what we held. With the truth still being buried or fought against, this now becomes the responsibility of anyone who reads the facts for themselves—having heard all, to know, and having done all, to stand.

Hogan's "Letter"—A Face-to-Face

Hogan, I got a chance to say goodbye to in person, not just on paper, in a moment that played out at the end of his life in a beautiful, grateful exchange.

When Hogan ran successfully in the Democratic primary, he was taken ill with a diagnosis of a brain tumor. I had rushed him to the hospital, made security arrangements, and asked Mary, his wife, permission to see him once she thought it appropriate. She assured me she would.

Many believed he had adopted me as a child. He and his wife had no children. We had a close professional relationship, you know the role he played in being my gateway into this life and giving me an example to follow, facing up to corruption in a way that would literally rewrite law in a historic time, and during a time of exceeding corruption. Plus I had prosecuted successfully to verdict more cases than anyone else, so I followed through on the path he paved.

It would be months before Mary would call, but when she did, she told me the time had come. I went immediately to the hospital. Mrs. Hogan showed me into the room where he was in extremely serious condition.

He held in his hands a Hogan's Hooligans office baseball team autographed ball. Mrs. Hogan told me to sit down by the bedside chair facing and close to him. I wasn't sure he knew I was in the room; he was murmuring and staring straight ahead. Nevertheless, I told him how much all of our ADA's missed him and were so looking forward to his return to the office. I was overwhelmingly sorrowful but wanted him to know that he was our moral leader and how much he meant to all of us. Because he did—just as much as if we were all still wandering in to his open door, with the lamplight and calls he would always personally pick up, and the "right calls" he would make, even if he had to stand against the world.

When I finished talking with him, I started getting up from my chair by placing my left hand on the bed's metal bar. Mr. Hogan grabbed my hand and placed it to his lips. He looked directly at me without saying a word. I nodded to him and thanked him again for all that he did for all of us, this time with my fisted hand over my heart. He smiled and nodded at me, dropped his head down towards his left shoulder, closed his eyes, and made no more movement.

He died a few days later.

Nothing would ever be the same.

No one could have expected any of this. From my coach tying on my sneakers, drill instructor though he was, to Hogan still holding the baseball, this was a company of warriors and a cloud of witnesses who always stood for truth and had no qualms saying it out loud, whatever the truth may be. All we knew was that it would set us free.

It's a tenet of the foundation of our nation and who we were meant to be as people. Generally, values are derived initially from our parents and experiences outside the family setting. Yet, as part of the American experience, history also plays a significant influence: In the seventeenth century, the Puritans and Scots-Irish emigrated to America. They both fled oppression and were fiercely independent. This is a key understanding that few have maintained in our current culture.

This founding emigration was not a legalistically fundamentalist society. On the contrary, this was a move of people with a fierce belief in freedom for all humankind and a shared a distrust of central government, believing that our precious individual rights presently contained in our Bill of Rights come from the hand of God, not the State! Government is only valid, they believed, if it acts with the consent of the governed.

From this history emerged the concept we shall be as a City on the Hill. Circa 1630, Massachusetts-bound John Winthrop, aboard the *Arbella* and sailing towards the New World, admonished his fellow colonists that we shall be as a City on the Hill and analogized his fellow colonists to the children of Israel in the Old Testament:

> *"We too are taking a perilous voyage, this one, across a vast ocean and believe that we are delivered by God to this new Promised Land."*

But Winthrop cautioned that,

> *If we deal falsely with our God, He shall punish us. His blessings depend not on our worldly striving but on our moral performance. Our security as well as our salvation lie in the proper care of our souls, not the acquisition or exercise of power."*

You see, American exceptionalism is not an American superiority concept at all; it's a moral concept and it's all part of this whole thing. Morality. The notion was, you will receive rewards for your moral courage and the manner in which you take care of your soul and your society. If you ever expect to have anything precious passed from on high down to you, that is the measurement. It's not about power; it's not about the worldly issues of power and money and high office. That's not what it's about.

Let me just emphasize that at this crucial turning point, because not only do I think this concept and potential personal

Evidentiary Culmination

calling (as an individual or as a community) will encourage many, but it's also a bit of a handing off of a baton. Some of these men hired me, I hired some of them, technically to jobs and appointed positions, but even more, it was an invitation to uphold truth and to make noise about it where it is being contaminated, demolished, or eradicated.

You can't teach honor, integrity, and loyalty. These are things that have to connect with you on their own. You can, however, enact them in a way that sparks a divine moral concept and purpose in someone else. You can pass on the strength and encouragement of your own example in a way that has momentum and is momentously consequential.

My family taught me this. My coaches drilled it into me. I watched the lack of it take others down and the want of it raise others to greatness. I watched Hogan be that pinnacle and never waver. I watched Sprague never falter. I watched the whole cast of characters define character and in so doing, define me and the direction of the wheels of justice.

We literally rewrote law through integral risks. Miranda exists. Boyle was convicted, while a salt-of-the-earth community of Appalachians was protected. And as sure as I stand here, or ever shot a few hoops, I swear to you, Lee Harvey Oswald did not kill JFK.

I've lived long enough to hand that Truth to you. What you do with it, my friend, is up to you.

Appendix 1
Truman Memo

Limit CIA Role To Intelligence

By Harry S. Truman

Copyright, 1963, by Harry S. Truman

THE WASHINGTON POST
Sunday, Dec. 22, 1963

operational + policy making

INDEPENDENCE, MO., Dec. 21 — I think it has become necessary to take another look at the purpose and operations of our Central Intelligence Agency—CIA. At least, I would like to submit here the original reason why I thought it necessary to organize this Agency during my Administration, what I expected it to do and how I expected it to operate as an arm of the President.

I think it is fairly obvious that by and large a President's performance in office is as effective as the information he has and the information he gets. That is to say, that assuming the President himself possesses a knowledge of our history, a sensitive understanding of our institutions, and an insight into the needs and aspirations of the people, he needs to have available to him the most accurate and up-to-the-minute information on what is going on everywhere in the world, and particularly of the trends and developments in all the danger spots in the contest between East and West. This is an immense task and requires a special kind of an intelligence facility.

Of course, every President has available to him all the information gathered by the many intelligence agencies already in existence. The Departments of State, Defense, Commerce, Interior and others are constantly engaged in extensive information gathering and have done excellent work.

But their collective information reached the President too frequently in conflicting conclusions. At times, the intelligence reports tended to be slanted to conform to established positions of a given department. This becomes confusing and what's worse, such intelligence is of little use to a President in reaching the right decisions.

Therefore, I decided to set up a special organization charged with the collection of all intelligence reports from every available source, and to have those reports reach me as President without departmental "treatment" or interpretations.

I wanted and needed the information in its "natural raw" state and in as comprehensive a volume as it was practical for me to make full use of it. But the most important thing about this move was to guard against the chance of intelligence being used to influence or to lead the President into unwise decisions—and I thought it was necessary that the President do his own thinking and evaluating.

Since the responsibility for decision making was his — information is kept from him for whatever reason at the pleasure of those who would want to shield a President from bad news or misjudgments to spare him from being "upset."

For some time I have been disturbed by the way CIA has been diverted from its original assignment. It has become an operational and at times a policy-making arm of the Government. This has led to trouble and may have compounded our difficulties in several explosive areas.

I never had any thought that when I set up the CIA that it would be injected into peacetime cloak and dagger operations. Some of the complications and embarrassment that I think we have experienced are in part attributable to the fact that this quiet intelligence arm of the President has been so removed from its intended role that it is being interpreted as a symbol of sinister and mysterious foreign intrigue—and a subject for cold war enemy propaganda.

With all the nonsense put out by Communist propaganda about "Yankee imperialism," "exploitive capitalism," "war mongering," "monopolists," in their name-calling assault on the West, the last thing we needed was for the CIA to be seized upon as something akin to a subverting influence in the affairs of other people.

I well knew the first temporary director of the CIA, Adm. Souers, and the later permanent directors of the CIA, Gen. Hoyt Vandenberg and Allen Dulles. These were men of the highest character, patriotism and integrity—and I assume this is true of all those who continue in charge.

But there are now some searching questions that need to be answered. I, therefore, would like to see the CIA be restored to its original assignment as the intelligence arm of the President, and that whatever else it can properly perform in that special field—and that its operational duties be terminated or properly used elsewhere.

We have grown up as a nation, respected for our free institutions and for our ability to maintain a free and open society. There is something about the way the CIA has been functioning that is casting a shadow over our historic position and I feel that we need to correct it.

(Souce: CIA Freedom of Information Act Electronic Reading Room. https://www.cia.gov/readingroom/docs/CIA-RDP75-00149R000700550045-9.pdf)

Appendix 2
McCone Letter

UNITED STATES GOVERNMENT

Memorandum

Mr. James J. Rowley
Chief, U S Secret Service

DATE March [...] 1964

Mr. John McCone
Director, Central Intelligence Agency

CO-2-34,030

SUBJECT: Central Intelligence Report on the Assassination of John Kennedy

In response to the request made by your office on 24 February 1964 re: Lee Oswald's activities and assignments on behalf of this agency and Federal Bureau of Investigation, there follows a narrative summary of the internal subversive activities of the Oswald subject.

I recommend that unless the Commission makes a specific request for specific information contained herein, that this information not be volunteered. This agency has reason to assume that some junior Commission staff members may be potential sources of leaks to the news media or to other agencies; due to the highly sensitive nature of the enclosed material, it would certainly be in the national interest to withhold it at this time - unless there is, of course, a specific request made.

It is my understanding that Mr. Hoover has certain sensitive information within his agency, which has been transferred to his own personal files for safekeeping; he concurs that no material should be voluntarily given to the Commission which might affect the status of field operatives or their safety. He is particularly concerned about the De Bruey memorandum, which Central Intelligence has obtained and which, I understand, you have obtained. It is imperative that this information, at least for the time, remain under wraps.

Oswald subject was trained by this agency, under cover of the Office of Naval Intelligence, for Soviet assignments. During preliminary training, in 1957, subject was active in aerial reconnaissance of mainland China and maintained a security clearance up to the "confidential" level. His military records during this period are open to your agency and I have directed they be forwarded to the Commission.

Subject received additional indoctrination at our own Camp Peary site from September 8 to October 17, 1958, and participated in a few relatively minor assignments until arrangements were made for his entry to the Soviet Union in September 1959. While in the Soviet Union, he was on special assignment in the area of Minsk, it would not be advantageous at this time to divulge the specifics of that assignment; however, if you wish this information, it can be made available for your personal inspection within the confines of our own offices, or I can send it by courier on the condition that it not leave the custody of the courier. I am concerned that if this information were in any way disclosed to the wrong persons it would lead the media to erroneously claim this agency and perhaps others, were directly involved in the Dallas action. While the persons involved were in the employ of this agency as well as the Federal Bureau of Investigation, it is virtually impossible for this or any agency to maintain full 24-hour-a-day responsibility over its operatives.

At the time of the Dallas action, the Oswald subject was only seldom in our employ; after the Soviet assignment, we found him to be unreliable and emotionally unstable. He was of little use to us after his marriage and De Bruey, from what I understand, concurs in this. He was provided with a few unimportant infiltration assignments and proved of little or no value.

It is possible that Oswald, given his instability, might have been involved in some operation concerning Hoffa, as noted in SAIC Bertram's report to your agency dated 1/3/64. Mr. Hoover advises that his agency is trying to determine whether Hoffa might have been involved laterally or vertically with the Dallas assassination. I have advised that I would be interested in seeing the results of that investigation.

Mr. Hoover advises that the facts given in SAIC Bertram's 1/3/64 report are basically correct; his agency has advised Deputy Sweatt against further unauthorized statements to the news media which might adversely effect the investigation. Mr. Hoover advises he has no knowledge of how Deputy Sweatt obtained his information, as there is no record of the agency distributing any such information to Sweatt or any other member of Dallas Sheriff's office. It is regrettable that this information has come to the attention of the news media, but I am sure Mr. Hoover will be able to clarify the situation.

Speculation within this agency – and this is only speculation at this point - is that the Oswald subject became unstable following surgery April 1, 1961, in the Minsk Hospital. He may have been chemically or electronically "controlled" ... a sleeper agent. Subject spent eleven days hospitalized for a "minor ailment" which should have required no more than three days hospitalization at the most. Six days after his release, he met Marina Prusakova. This agency is particularly interested in her intelligence background, and I have requested a report on same from our Soviet Embassy contact.

After his return to the U.S., Oswald worked in New Orleans through The Anti-Communist League of the Caribbean and Friends of Democratic Cuba, his case officer was SAIC Guy Bannister, from the Chicago FBI office. He was transferred from his assignments there after he was arrested and fined for an incident stemming from his distribution of pamphlets for the Fair Play for Cuba Committee. While our files here show no further assignments or contact, I am requesting an A5 check on the subject from our New Orleans and Ft. Worth offices.

CONFIDENTIAL

Please direct any further communications on this matter to my personal attention so that your requests may be expedited, or feel free to call me anytime. My office is always available to you.

Appendix 3
Rangers at Pointe du Hoc

"The Rangers looked up and saw the enemy soldiers -- the edge of the cliffs shooting down at them with machine guns and throwing grenades. And the American Rangers began to climb. They shot rope ladders over the face of these cliffs and began to pull themselves up. When one Ranger fell, another would take his place. When one rope was cut, a Ranger would grab another and begin his climb again. They climbed, shot back, and held their footing. Soon, one by one, the Rangers pulled themselves over the top, and in seizing the firm land at the top of these cliffs, they began to seize back the continent of Europe. Two hundred and twenty-five came here. After two days of fighting, only 90 could still bear arms.

These are the boys of Pointe du Hoc. These are the men who took the cliffs. These are the champions who helped free a continent. These are the heroes who helped end a war.

The Americans who fought here that morning knew word of the invasion was spreading through the darkness back home. They felt in their hearts, though they couldn't know in fact, that in Georgia they were filling the churches at 4 a.m., in Kansas they were kneeling on their porches and praying, and in Philadelphia they were ringing the Liberty Bell.

These are the things that impelled them; these are the things that shaped the unity of the Allies."

– Excerpts from President Ronald Reagan's speech commemorating the 40th Anniversary of the D-Day invasion and The Boys of Pointe du Hoc, June 6, 1984

"Behind me is a memorial that symbolizes the Ranger daggers that were thrust into the top of these cliffs. And before me are the men who put them there."

– President Ronald Reagan

About the Author

Robert K. Tanenbaum is the author of thirty-three books—twenty-nine novels, featuring Butch Karp and Marlene Ciampi, and four nonfiction books: *Badge of the Assassin*, *The Piano Teacher*, *Echoes of My Soul*, and *Coal Country Killing*. He is one of the most successful prosecuting attorneys, having never lost a felony trial and convicting hundreds of violent criminals. He was a special prosecution consultant on the Hillside strangler case in Los Angeles and defended Amy Grossberg in her sensationalized baby death case. He was Assistant District Attorney in New York County in the office of legendary District Attorney Frank Hogan, where he ran the Homicide Bureau, served as Chief of the Criminal Courts, and was in charge of the DA's legal staff training program. He served as Deputy Chief Counsel for the Congressional Committee investigation into the assassinations of President John F. Kennedy and the Rev. Dr. Martin Luther King, Jr.

Tanenbaum also served two terms as mayor of Beverly Hills and taught Advanced Criminal Procedure for four years at Boalt Hall School of Law, University of California, Berkeley. He has conducted continuing legal education (CLE) seminars for practicing lawyers in California, New York, and Pennsylvania. Born in Brooklyn, New York, he attended the University of California at Berkeley, on a basketball scholarship, where he earned a BA and received his law degree (JD) from UC Berkeley Boalt Hall School of Law.

Visit: https://robertktanenbaumbooks.com

READER'S NOTES

READER'S NOTES

READER'S NOTES

READER'S NOTES

READER'S NOTES

READER'S NOTES

READER'S NOTES

READER'S NOTES

READER'S NOTES

READER'S NOTES